A MIDHURST LAD

A Sussex childhood from the mid 1920s to the late 1930s

Ronald E. Boxall

LARGE PRINT
Oxford

First published in Great Britain 2003
by

Pu   .td,

Gloucestershire County
Council

British Library Cataloguing in Publication Data
Boxall, Ronald E., 1924–
    A Midhurst lad. – Large print ed.
    (Isis reminiscence series)
    1. Boxall, Ronald E., 1924– – Childhood and youth
    2. Large type books
    3. Sussex (England) – Social life and customs
    4. Midhurst (England) – Biography
    I. Title
    942.2'62083'092

ISBN 0–7531–9320–5 (hb)
ISBN 0–7531–9321–3 (pb)

Printed and bound in Great Britain by
T. J. International Ltd., Padstow, Cornwall

Contents

To my mother and my friend, Charles Bowyer

My mother credits me with an exceptionally good memory; not so much concerning my adult life (I forget more recent events just as easily as the next man), but mostly for my recollections of early childhood, even babyhood, for my train of memories here recorded begins in the confines of a pram.

Over the years Mother has often put me to the test by asking me to recount various incidents related to my early days. In many cases she has been agreeably surprised at my responses. "Well I never," she would say, "I'd forgotten about that bit, myself."

My venerable old friend, Charles Bowyer, a man blessed with a superb memory, as all who know him will agree, has complimented me by declaring that, even as a young man, he could not recall his childhood days with anything like the clarity with which I am able to recount mine. We are, however, agreed that one's childhood — even viewed from advanced middle age — seems by far the longest part of one's life. Yet in the telling of many a life story those early days are all too often a truly condensed part of the tale.

There is nothing outstanding about my early years. I have merely recorded most of what I remember about the average life of an average boy born of poor parents, who, at one time, lived under slum conditions, yet dwelt in the very centre of a tiny and pretty town set in a near paradise of pastoral and sylvan delights.

My story stems from this twin environment. It is an autobiography, which deals with my childhood only; a sequence of events that spans little more than one decade — from the middle 1920s to the late 1930s.

To those who read it I trust it will convey a view of the world as seen through the eyes of almost any child of that period born into a lowly strata of human society. Moreover, I trust it will succeed in wakening many a sleeping memory in the minds of those who find pleasure in looking over their shoulder.

My mother and my friend, Charles Bowyer, both octogenarians, instilled in me the urge to write my tale. Wholeheartedly, I thank them for their encouragement. I hope they enjoy my story as much as I enjoyed writing it, and to them I dedicate it, most gratefully.

Ronald E. Boxall, 1983

Introduction to Duck Lane

It seems that one moment I was lying peacefully in my pram in a condition of sleepy, infantile indifference, when, in a trice, I was transported into a painful state of awareness.

The pram was rocking violently and leaning dangerously to one side. Vicious white fangs, set in a huge face, were snapping at my unresisting knuckles. Since my powers of imagination were, as yet, undeveloped, the spectacle in itself held no fears for me. The pain in my hand did.

Fortunately, my four-year-old sister did not pursue her cannibalistic tendencies for more than a few seconds, but I recall giving forth a scream, which was — probably for the first time — induced neither by hunger nor wind. Suddenly the hostile face was gone, to be replaced immediately by an even larger one; but this was a countenance of kindness, which I was to look to for many years as a source of understanding and panacea for all fears and ills, and one which I was soon to identify with the word "Mama".

Her voice rang out, in reprimand no doubt, and I heard the sound of crying. Then came a cooing, comforting babble, all directed at me. I was drifting into oblivion again, but my first memory was born.

I had been born many months earlier, in the year 1924, at an address, which was then synonymous with poverty. I first saw the shadowy light of day at Duck Lane in the middle of the otherwise attractive town of Midhurst, an old market place, small and neat, reposing comfortably in a velvety green valley of West Sussex.

Today, more than fifty years on, Duck Lane remains a narrow, L-shaped byway, linking two main thoroughfares of the town. The overall length is about one hundred and fifty yards. The leg of the L rises gradually from its junction with West Street, then following an abrupt left turn, the foot descends sharply to meet at a right angle the upper sweep of North Street.

At various points along its entire length it provides access to the rear premises of a number of shops. Its position and function remains unaltered, but it is now a much renovated and, indeed, quaint-looking quarter. At the time of my birth it was a stretch of stone-built, whitewashed squalor, of which my story requires a full description.

Moving into Duck Lane from West Street one beheld on either side a confusion of rickety old buildings and rather untidy backyards, which, taken as a whole, contained all manner of mercantile attributes. And always in this quarter, there was a subtle yet all pervading scent, an odorous diffusion of chiefly fish and paraffin. Farther on the lane narrowed; the left-hand side still bordered upon backyards, but to the right, hard to the roadside, there ran a tall stone-built wall. This in turn gave way to what might best be described as a row of tiny hovels.

Seven in number and all attached they made up an overall outline, which suggested that at least one storey had sunk beneath the ground. This was due to the roof, which swept down to a level only just above the front door lintels. From this roof, jutting out at regular intervals, were seven small dormer windows, rather like a row of elevated dog kennels.

Along the length of the building ran a narrow pavement surmounted at the foot of each shabby door by a single stone step. Each dwelling contained one lower front window, small, with its tiny panes gazing, with little to reflect, across the strip of road at a high stone wall. This was the boundary enclosing the backyard of the International Grocers Store, and it was flanked by old and mostly derelict buildings. The wall, together with the buildings, occupied a position that ensured the sun must ever set early upon that row of pitiful dwellings.

Nearing the top end of this line of hovels, one's attention was drawn to a low, open passageway that ran between the ground floors of numbers five and six. This led to a small area of waste ground, which nestled behind the last two cottages, and where clotheslines and Y-shaped wooden props indicated its use as a communal drying ground.

On the far side of the drying ground, reached by a broad cement path that ran on from the passage, was a flight of stone steps, some four or five feet wide, which, rising to a similar height, presented one upon the threshold of a little forecourt. To its left stood an attached pair of houses. The whole of this area, both below and above the steps, was surrounded by tall, bleak walls, butted against the back gardens of far more prosperous homes standing upon higher ground, but concealed from view by those same walls.

The two cottages at the top of the steps were little better than those in the lane. They were all minus bathrooms, electricity and indoor toilets, but, at least, these homes did have the advantage of just a little more daylight.

The interior of each dwelling in the lane was much the same. The front door opened directly into a tiny living room. Almost immediately opposite was a middle door that led to a cement-paved scullery from which a heavy back door opened onto a narrow strip of concrete. On the near side was ranged a diversified array of rusting receptacles, all in use as dustbins, and each standing by its allotted door.

The far side of the path was bordered by a towering wall, some twelve feet high or more; its close proximity to the rear of the building effectually created an impression of perpetual twilight. This was with the happy exception of hovels six and seven: they looked out over the drying ground. Since each scullery boasted one tiny, square window, there was a period every morning — should the skies be clear — when the rear interiors of these two end cottages were graced by the presence of a sunbeam or two.

On the right of the drying ground, beneath yet another very high wall, stood the primitive water closets — each looking ancient enough to qualify as the prototype of flush toilets. They were housed in a shed-like construction containing four compartments. Four lavatories serving, in all, nine families.

In spite of the vigorous efforts of the hygienically-minded, the degenerate habits manifested by some of the more primeval occupants prompted me, at a very young age, to make the observation that, as long as one did not have a cold, the lavatories were to be easily found without the aid of a light on the darkest of nights.

In each compartment the seating accommodation was without frills; strictly utilitarian, in the form of a box-like structure placed along the rear wall with a circular hole in the top centre.

One of my very early upsets was to occur in one of these compartments when, having completed my mission, I found that somehow my hindquarters had become firmly wedged in the hole. My rear end had sunk so low that I was stuck in a most ignominious position, legs splayed upwards, rather like the handles of a wheelbarrow, while my little fingers clawed at the seat in a desperate attempt to gain sufficient purchase to lever myself free. I failed completely, and so I screamed for what seemed to me an eternity until a young girl arrived upon the scene and quite painlessly extricated me. I had been scared, but fortunately I was far too young to feel any embarrassment.

I was born at number three, Duck Lane, in the upstairs room. I use the singular because each dwelling possessed only one real bedroom. It was situated above the living room and was reached by means of a dogleg staircase, which snaked up from the scullery to a landing at the rear of the building. The bedroom was through a low door to the right at the head of the stairway. In the bedroom the ceiling adhered to the slope of the roof. Set in the skilling[1] was a dormer window, which allowed for an edifying prospect of the backyard belonging to the International Grocers Store.

The room was tiny, but when it came to furnishings few could afford more than bare necessities, so this was considered to be of no great disadvantage. Indeed, where there was a family of four of more, the installation of two beds, with the parents in one and an offspring or two in the other was the usual arrangement. This overcrowded situation was more easily acceptable during a cold spell for, with no means of heating, it did create a roost-like warmth. In these cramped conditions, especially with children in mind, few people cared to use the rather dangerous and malodorous portable oil stoves of that period.

---

[1] *Skilling*: a word much used in the Midhurst meaning *a sharply sloping ceiling, which adhered to the line of the roof*. (Author)

The landing was a fortuitous result of architectural ineptitude; what was little more than a platform — the underside of which provided the scullery with a ceiling — became, because of dire overcrowding in growing families, an open bedroom. It was quite big enough to contain a bed, but, being even narrower than the bedroom proper, the sloping ceiling afforded moments of extreme consternation. A not-all-too-rare example was to wake from slumber and forgetting the proximity of the skilling, attempt to sit up in the bed. The result, of course, was to thump one's head against the plaster or, worse, one of the supporting rafters.

At the foot of the bed was a narrow continuation of the landing, which served to cover the well of the staircase. This and the stairway itself, was by day the best-lit area in the entire hovel, for in the ceiling immediately above was a skylight — a window, which looked uninterrupted to the heavens. There was at times an exception to this continuity; a fall of snow would completely negate its function.

In our house the area of landing, which reached out from the foot of the bed, was utilised purely in the interest of Bacchus. It was here that row upon row of bottles, all loosely corked and containing many varieties of homemade wine, bubbled away in various stages of fermentation. It was a wine-bedecked altar from which emanated, day and night, a sibilant anthem to Bacchus with, perhaps, a thanksgiving hymn thrown in, glorifying the wine gods of Sussex. These wines were revered by the neighbours, enjoyed by all, and much tasted by me: albeit, in my younger days, mostly through a finger-licking process.

So it was, in this environment, I began to outgrow my pram.

CHAPTER ONE

Early Memories

I was not quite three when I paid my first visit to a hospital, the Royal West Sussex, at nearby Chichester. On the way to this establishment I was terribly travelsick, vomiting willy-nilly all over the conductor's platform at the rear of the bus. He was very good about it, and I remember that he handed me very gently to my mother after she had alighted — although it was at arm's length and cautiously pointed outwards.

Totally unsuspecting I was to be operated upon for an inguinal hernia, which my parents were convinced was brought about by the fairly recent acquisition of a pedal-car.

This car, the unwanted toy of a more privileged family, was brought to me on a memorable day by my father. I will never forget the terrible length of that particular day, for I had been told what he was going to bring me upon his return from work. All afternoon I kept a constant vigil, asking my mother a score of times just how much longer was there to wait. Then I saw him as he turned in from West Street. Carrying the car high upon his shoulder he strode towards me and, in that never to be forgotten moment, I ran dangerously fast to meet him. He lowered the car and placed me in the driving seat. I was fairly bursting with excitement and this wonderful, blue pedal-car was to remain my pride and joy for a very long time.

In those days wheeled traffic in Duck Lane was an infrequent intrusion. I recall that a milkman arrived twice daily with a pony and trap, and the dustcart, pulled by a gigantic grey horse, once a week. The lamplighter man, who carried a long pole and rode a bicycle, came every morning and evening. There were a few irregular deliveries made by motor vans, but mobility in the lane was mostly pedestrian — until the arrival of my little car.

At this very moment my grandmother, more popularly called Nan, opened her front door. Her instant appraisal differed only on a point of priority, for she saw more at risk than just a blue pedal-car. For a twinkling she looked at me horrified, then rushing forward she pulled both me and my car to safety. She then cried out to my uncles who appeared almost at once upon the forecourt to be told excitedly of my accomplishment. Astonishment gave way to admiration and, although I was moderately admonished for my somewhat reckless undertaking, there was no doubt that I was the hero of the day.

By then my uncles were relating my feat of strength to a few neighbours who had been attracted to the scene by the commotion. It was a moment of absolute triumph. I climbed into the car and, pedalling furiously, I did a couple of laps of honour.

Nan then took me and the car, for I would not leave it, into her little front room where she plied me with my then favourite delicacy, sweetened condensed milk spread on fingers of bread. This was followed, by my own special request, with several spoonfuls of soft brown sugar. Uncle Harry then came in and presented me with a small bar of milk chocolate.

Now all of this kind attention was to eventually prove deleterious to me for, ever mindful of the mouth-watering rewards, I was to repeat the climb — burdened with the car — on more than one occasion. Obviously, Nan was aware of my ulterior motives for in every respect the encouragement ceased. Indeed, upon reflection, a vainglorious period followed my first success for I received little more than reproof for all subsequent endeavours. I will never know which attempt caused the rupture.

I was lying in a cot and looking up at a ceiling that seemed as high as the sky itself. Uniformed ladies were cluck-clucking at me, at the same time handing me cuddly toys of all descriptions. Most of these were inanimate animals that I threw in my uncontrollable rage to the floor. I was crying as loudly as I could, and I was determined to go on crying until my mother returned to take me away from this huge, strange place.

I must have pushed all of the nurses and most of the patients — young though the latter were — to a point of exasperation, when I was suddenly hushed by the appearance of yet another toy. Joyful incredulity was displayed in the smile of the nurse who had proffered this latest fortuitous peace offering. She had unwittingly produced an amazingly effective mollification. The toy I clutched was a tiny blue-painted, metal car. Lovingly I held it to me and then quite exhausted I fell asleep.

The impact of separation from all that I knew so well seemed to end at this juncture. I have vague memories of playing within the confines of my cot, mostly with the little blue car, and of being fed on several occasions, but not more than one clear recollection pertaining to the purpose of my visit.

This one recollection projects a scene in which my lower anatomy is a focal point. A bevy of nurses is gathered around my cot; each member is paying a great deal of interest to an area below my waistline. At the same time they secure my limbs with gentle but firm hands. Fascinated, I watch the particular hand, which operates what appears to be a pair of scissors in the region of my groin. Assuming I was then witnessing the removal of stitches, this then was the final stage of a completely successful piece of surgery.

Even at that time, a hernia repair was not considered to be a dangerous operation, but it was an age of antiseptics not antibiotics and I imagine, therefore, that everyone concerned breathed a sigh of relief once it was seen that I had made a good recovery. Already I had lost an elder brother and a younger sister, both in infancy — neither of whom I remember — to commonplace illnesses such as pneumonia and whooping cough.

I feel that I might well have been in a less sturdy condition when I left the hospital than when I arrived, for I do not recall the homeward trip with anything like the clarity with which I remember the outward journey.

I also feel that for a time after my arrival home I was kept very quiet, and that this uneventful confinement created a void from which I seem to spring, and to come alive again periodically and quite abruptly.

There follows a series of events, disjointed in all respects, but nevertheless well remembered, probably because of their isolation.

In one instance, I was sitting on the floor in the scullery watching Mother laundering in the low shallow sink. She placed a bowl on the floor and I observed how she dipped the clothes in and out of the water before wringing them out preparatory to winding them through the big, heavy mangle.

Near the bowl stood the dog's basket. It was a bitch for I recall there were three or four very young puppies tucked away in this basket. Where the bitch was at the time I never knew, but for some reason Mother was called away for a few minutes, and it was then that I decided to wash the puppies. One by one I popped them into the bowl. They struggled frantically as I dipped first one and then another under the surface, rubbing and wringing them out just as Mother had done with the clothes.

Happily, she returned just in time, and only just. She grabbed them from the water and swiftly applied some form of artificial respiration. Miraculously all survived, though one small heap of soggy fur remained on the danger list for at least a couple of days.

Another isolated memory is of a heinous crime for which I received my first experience of corporal punishment. Had I committed such a nefarious offence some seventeen years on I, doubtless, would have incurred a more serious penalty through a court of judicial procedure.

The crime most certainly took place at around Christmas; paper-chains festooned the ceiling above the table at which I sat, resting comfortably upon Uncle Mossy's lap. There were several other grown-ups seated around the table, but time has erased most of the detail.

What I do remember most vividly is pulling hard at my uncle's bushy moustache with one hand whilst with the other I grasped a sharp knife and drew it, quite effectively, across his throat. Blood spurted all over the place and I found myself in a heap upon the floor as poor Uncle Mossy rushed to the scullery sink. Mother grabbed the knife from me, and justly inflicted the said slaps before scuttling off to render assistance to my victim.

I was crying loudly, but I could still hear the hullabaloo around the table high above me. I decided, probably through fear of further reprisals, to move as far as possible from such hostile company. I crawled a yard or so and then, sitting upon the homemade rag mat in front of the fireplace, I glared somewhat huffishly at all the faces looking down at me. The memory fades with a mental picture of Uncle Mossy finishing his meal with a white, bloodstained towel wrapped tightly around his neck.

Uncle Mossy features in yet another short and stark memory. I was in the front room and he and my father were having a blazing row in the scullery. I had no clue as to what it was all about, nor do I know to this day who threw the first punch, but curiosity drew me to the open doorway just as Father caught Uncle Mossy with a beautiful right hook smack on the point of the jaw. Down went Uncle like a log, his head narrowly missing the heavy iron gas stove.

I was still wide eyed with this thrilling introduction to fisticuffs when along came Mother and helped poor Uncle to his feet, remonstrating with both men as she did so. Father, who had done so well in the physical conflict, seemed completely outclassed by Mother's verbal onslaught. It was not long before the two men shook hands and they never again fell out.

About this time a kind man with a lorry provided Father, Uncle Mossy and me with a day's outing. He took us all of twelve miles or more to a place called Pulborough where we visited a cattle market. After an interesting morning we set out for home pulling up at about the halfway mark in order to meet another great-uncle of mine who lived thereabouts. The convenient rendezvous was a public house, which I now know was near the wood in which my uncle lived.

We sat on a bench outside the inn, I with a little glass of lemonade, the men with very big mugs of beer. Suddenly, Uncle Mossy spluttered and coughed and swore, spilling his beer all over the place. He had been stung near the back of his tongue by a wasp; in fact, at the point where tongue meets throat. I thought the wasp was the more unlucky, for I saw Uncle Mossy, having spat out the offending insect, stamp heavily upon it as it lay helpless in a pool of beer.

I have since learned that Uncle Mossy suffered a great deal of pain followed by acute discomfort over the next few days. Looking back at the vicissitudes of poor Uncle Mossy, it would seem that Dame Fortune seldom smiled upon him.

Only three other events do I recall vividly at this stage of my life. One is the fairly regular magic lantern show put on by our immediate neighbours at Duck Lane. The ghostly images were projected onto the door at the foot of the stairs in their scullery. I was a little wary of these strange apparitions, but I think I was rather more puzzled than scared.

The second took place in the front room of another neighbour, where a cat's whisker wireless receiver puzzled not only me, but also most of the grown-ups in Duck Lane at some time. I spent quite a number of interesting spells in that little front room.

The third memory is slightly less vivid, possibly because there was no repetition. It is of being in the company of several grown-ups in the back of a noisy motor-van. We were on a trip to the seaside, and it was a very bumpy ride, for the tyres were of solid rubber. Strangely enough, I do not recall much about the seaside, only the journey there and back. Long afterwards I learned that we had visited East Wittering, a distance of some eighteen miles, and that the van was called "A Trojan".

Memories, although remaining as islands in the stream of time, began to lengthen, and my first of any length encompassed the whole of one day. I spent this particular day with Aunt Kate, my father's sister who lived less than half a mile from Duck Lane. I have no idea why I was placed there for the day, but it was a beautiful morning and I was enjoying it immensely.

At the back of Aunt Kate's house was a long garden, at the far end of which stood a sty accommodating two enormous pigs. Next to this was a run for the chickens, from whose little house I had earlier collected several very warm eggs. Bouncing around in a small aviary were a few pretty but squeaky budgerigars. There were two white mice in a cage, and a black cat and a brown dog prowled their own ways around the garden, all contributed to a fascinating display of domesticated animal life.

But the most thrilling specimen of them all was a big, very tame jackdaw, truly beloved by my aunt. Despite complete freedom, whenever she was in the backyard or the garden it seldom flew very far from her side.

She called it Jack, an unimaginative, but effective name; it responded to it with alacrity, and loved to

17

perch upon her shoulder, its head cocked to one side, receiving her soft caresses while listening to her murmured endearments. Jack would then reciprocate by rubbing his head fondly against her ear, before giving forth a squawking protestation of love — at least that was Aunt Kate's interpretation of his vociferous outburst.

It remained a lovely day. The weather was hot, but to me this was superfluous, for I was aglow with excitement the whole time. Whenever the animals needed to be fed I was at Aunt Kate's side ready to help. With a big spade, and a little assistance from her, I even buried a dead rat, which she had earlier removed from a trap concealed somewhere in the chicken run. So must be the fate of all unwanted visitors she explained.

In late afternoon Aunt Kate was up at the house preparing the evening meal. I was still in the garden standing upon a pile of logs and leaning over the side of the sty watching the pigs as they grubbed around exploring the pungent smelling earth with their long snouts.

A sudden commotion, including my aunt's voice, had me running towards the house. Close to the back door, in the little yard where the white mice and budgerigars lived, Aunt Kate was beating with a heavy stick at what appeared to be an empty sack. But no, as I came upon the scene, sharp convulsions from its interior brought yet another rain of blows upon it. The battering continued until there was no more movement from within.

Panting heavily, my aunt gingerly raised the bottom corners of the sack.

"Here's another rat for you to bury," she said, and began to shake the grim contents to the ground. Out fell the pulped and bloody remains of poor Jack, recognisable only by its feathers.

There were still tears in Aunt Kate's eyes when my mother arrived to take me home.

CHAPTER
TWO

Hard Times

Most of the homes in Duck Lane spilled over, prima facie, only with human beings, but there were other inhabitants who occupied the even darker recesses of the gloomy interiors. First, there were the fat and shiny black beetles whose community centre in each house lay in the murky depths of the coal cupboard situated in the scullery, partly under the stairs.

These intrepid creatures loved to walk abroad, but mainly in the dark. Most children considered it great fun to enter an unlit room and, suddenly striking a match, to watch and even listen to them as they scuttled away to less hazardous, and less illuminated, surroundings. It was, no doubt, for similar reasons that one might discover a beetle sharing one's bed: a not uncommon occurrence, which created no great alarm.

Then there were the fleas, smaller, but insidious insects which colonised somewhere in the stone walls beneath bulging plaster and layers of wallpaper. Keating's Powder was the first domestic pesticide I remember, and this I saw used in copious quantities, but I declare — perhaps with tongue in cheek — that a lot of these fleas built up an immunity to it, for it was not long before they were on the rampage again.

That the fleas did not like Keating's Powder was obvious, and funny at times, for if it were used against a dividing wall between two houses it had the effect of driving the main body into the neighbours' quarters. They would be quite understanding about it, but of course they would be forced to retaliate, and so it became a never-ending campaign.

Small wonder then that we kids of Duck Lane encountered and suffered all the infectious and contagious diseases more readily associated with the slum areas of industrial cities.

We were country children, living in the very heart of a market town set in beautiful surroundings. But it was a heart ravaged by time and neglect. I had so far been lucky, but early in my fourth year I contracted scarlet fever.

I was taken to an isolation hospital at Brighton, over thirty miles away, where I was to remain for several weeks. I think I must have been quite ill, for I recall very little about it. Only one clear memory comes to me. It is of my parents looking at me through a ward window. After a long, uncomfortable bus ride, to say nothing of the expense, they were not, of course, permitted any physical contact with me. All else is very hazy, but frequently for the greater part of my life I was to be reminded of this once dreaded disease by subsequent and recurrent ear trouble.

★   ★   ★

Following my recovery from scarlet fever, the early form of disjointed memories was gradually succeeded by recollections of a more closely linked, day-by-day sequence.

My favourite day was Sunday, when, forsaking the pleasures of my pedal-car, I toddled along towards Nan's house where Uncle Harry, a stocky and jovial man, always seemed to be waiting to see me safely up the steps. He would then usher me into the little front room, where, in the warmth of a glowing fire contained in a black and highly polished cooking range, we sang hymns. Upon reflection, I fear that my uncle's repertoire of hymns was somewhat limited, for "Oh God, our help in ages past" seemed to play a major part in each performance.

Despite this pious prelude, the tenet "Turn the other cheek" was certainly not one to which Uncle Harry would subscribe. For, immediately after the final "Amen", we would don boxing gloves: a pair of small, nearly new ones for me — although for a long time they were really too large and cumbersome — and for my uncle a tatty old pair of full-sized gloves.

Most times, weather permitting and with Uncle Harry upon his knees, we would battle it out on the forecourt, alongside the very low parapet that overlooked the drying ground; very often to the cheers and boos of watching neighbours, both young and old.

Always, as a conclusion to the bout, my uncle would coax such a blow from me that it would seem to lift him clear over the parapet and he would fall, apparently unconscious, to the ground below. Sometimes at this point there were hilarious scenes, as one or two adult spectators rushed to his aid, picking him up and rendering pseudo first aid with many exaggerated gestures. They would then assist him up the steps as he moaned and groaned, and swayed and staggered in a most realistic manner. I enjoyed every minute of it, especially when my hand was raised in victory, but I knew he was only kidding.

The third and final stage of the Sunday morning programme was equally enjoyable. Uncle Harry and I would first have a "wash and brush up" in the little scullery, and then, strolling hand in hand, we left Duck Lane and — in my case with mouth-watering anticipation — made our way to a nearby inn called the Wheatsheaf.

Here we separated, for I was always taken by the very nice landlord to a private room. From the doorway I was able to observe my uncle as he leaned against a counter, talking with lots of men all quaffing, it seemed, much needed refreshment. At the same time he kept a watchful eye upon me.

I was usually allowed just one chocolate wafer: a meagre offering I thought. But bearing in mind the time of day it was obviously limited to one in order to preserve my appetite for the dinner soon to follow. The lemonade, however, was never in short supply; it was yellow and indescribably delicious.

Then it was time to leave.

"Mustn't be late, for our sake," was Uncle Harry's usual comment as we left the Wheatsheaf, remembering

Nan's regular and imperious warning, "One o'clock, or else . . ."

He would first take me home before making his way up the steps to Nan's house where he enjoyed a well-deserved dinner with her and Uncle Mossy.

Uncle Mossy, too, spent a lot of time with me. He used to take me on long walks from which I invariably returned riding high upon his shoulders, and absolutely fagged out.

I was to learn, as I grew older, that he was unable to work for a living as the result of a war wound sustained somewhere in Mesopotamia — "Mespot" he used to call it. A near-spent Turkish bullet had struck him in the forehead and rendered him unconscious for more than a week. He was lucky to be alive, and in his forehead there was a depression under which a metal plate replaced the shattered bone. Dame Fortune smiled enigmatically. Exertion of a too vigorous nature would cause him to suffer from both giddiness and headache. In consequence, his sole income was by way of a small disability pension.

My father, too, bore war wounds. He had served in the Infantry in France, and was riddled with shrapnel. Twice during my childhood he underwent surgery in order to have the more troublesome fragments removed, for many of these pieces of metal refused to remain in one place, some of them creating problems and at times a lot of pain.

He had also a persistent cough, violent sometimes, which he firmly maintained was the result of having been subjected to poison gas. My mother said he smoked too much.

Uncle Harry had also served in the army, but a chest condition prevented him going overseas. There had been three brothers; Uncle William was killed at the Battle of Jutland.

Most of the manual workers, when not in their Sunday best, showed in their attire traces of their service life, especially in winter when greatcoats and puttees were a boon to the outdoor worker. My father worked mainly as a bricklayer's labourer and, when he was lucky enough to be in employment, upon his arrival home at the end of the day, it was my job to unwind his puttees and then to roll them up, very neatly, in readiness for the next morning.

More frequent periods of unemployment were already heralding the steady approach of a great depression and it was during one such period that Father suffered a nasty accident.

The weather was at the time intensely cold, and Father spent most of the daylight hours with his big twin-handled saw sawing logs on the sawhorse, which he kept in a far corner of the drying ground. He had, no doubt, infringed a few medieval forestry laws by gathering his winter's fuel from the Lord Of The Manor's local woodlands and common land, especially if it were green wood. And he was certainly jeopardising

25

his right to unemployment benefit for, having duly provided his own family with means of heating he would continue to produce logs of a popular size, which he would easily sell to more fortunate and, it was to be hoped, discreet people. A sack of average size, completely filled, would cost one shilling.

Father was not alone in his endeavour to supplement the pittance referred to as "dole money". Many other fellow creatures were engaged in a variety of surreptitious enterprises, and these projects were not born of a cardinal sin; with children to fend for, and a bitter winter to combat, they were brought about by a necessity bordering on desperation.

One of our neighbours, another unemployed man who lived at number seven, the end house in our row, had been watching my father sawing away in freezing conditions, and he made a remark regarding the dangers of cutting ice-encrusted wood. He was justified, for with the initial incision there was a marked tendency for the saw to strike off the icy surface and to bounce towards the hand that steadied the wood.

Swift reflex action had so far preserved Father's hand. Then it happened. Alas, on this baleful occasion the hand remained gripping the log as the jagged saw-teeth all but severed the thumb.

I was indoors, playing on the scullery floor, when they brought him in. Uncle Harry was supporting him, and the man whose warning had been ignored was intent upon holding the thumb in a near normal position.

Blood was spurting everywhere as they steered poor Father towards the sink. Turning the tap on they washed the wound in ice-cold water; it was then that I glimpsed the thumb hanging limply at an unfamiliar angle.

I clearly remember Father, grey-faced and swaying slightly, but with his good hand he retained a grip upon the rim of the sink and remained upright. Mother arrived from nowhere, as mothers are wont to do, and produced what appeared to be a white pillowcase, which was bound very tightly around the hand. I suppose it was too badly cut for them to bandage it properly.

Uncle Harry took charge, "Come on, Jack. Let's get you to a doctor." With the injured hand held high, the two men half carried Father through our little front room, out into the lane and away to the surgery that, fortunately, was very near the North Street end of Duck Lane. There my father received immediate attention and apparently everyone concerned was to be complimented.

For a long time the hand remained enveloped in a huge bandage, but the end result was a complete success. In fact, people with more than average surgical knowledge regarded it as a fantastic success. The operation had been performed by none other than the dispenser, there being no doctor on hand at the time.

It was Uncle Harry who kept the home fire burning for us during the rest of that bitter winter.

CHAPTER
THREE

Birth and Death

Since my sister's hostile appearance at my pram side, she does not feature greatly in my early memories. The reason, I have since learned, was that at the age of six poor Daisy was smitten by a very severe attack of scarlet fever, and had spent an inordinately long time at the Brighton isolation hospital. Although she received a lengthy period of treatment for an ensuing ear infection, the condition eventually called for surgery and she had undergone a totally successful operation for mastoiditis.

Daisy, at this stage of my story, had been made a temporary ward of a next-door family, for there was to be, very shortly, an addition made to ours.

I was four years' old, and on this chilly and still dark October morning I waited with my father in the soft glow of the oil lamp, which lit our tiny front room, for the arrival of a baby.

Through the bars in the centre of the gleaming, black iron, cooking range the fire was burning brightly, while on the hob to one side the big kettle was singing incessantly.

I was highly excited; I believe Father was too, for he drank lots of tea, and all the time he puffed clouds of smoke from his thin hand-rolled cigarettes. He frequently called up the stairs to my mother who, strangely enough, seemed fairly unconcerned. Indeed, she showed no apparent interest at all. Even when the nurse arrived with the baby, Mother remained upstairs in bed.

The nurse, with Father's assistance, brought her bicycle right into the front room, where it was inclined, looking rather out of place, against the sideboard — not, I might add, an expensive piece of furniture.

The baby, Father explained, was concealed in a black bag, which the nurse produced from a wooden box fixed to the rear carrier of the bicycle.

"May I see it?" I asked.

"Mother first," smiled the nurse and she took the baby upstairs.

Later that morning I was introduced to my little, and rather scrawny looking, brother.

He was duly baptised in the name of Cecil, and as time progressed it was accepted that he was not endowed with even a mildly efficient stomach. On occasions he was unable to ingest food in any form and there were times that, having successfully swallowed some kind of nutriment, he would promptly retch and disgorge it. In consequence, he was a seedy child, miserable and tiny, whose appearance caused many folk to air doubts regarding his chances of attaining puberty.

He was to prove them wrong. Despite many visits to hospitals all over the place — some of lengthy duration including one to Great Ormond Street, London, where we were told both his oesophagus and stomach were stretched by way of corrective treatment — he was to reach not only puberty but healthy adulthood.

Although his survival, so far as our family was concerned, kept the child mortality statistics fractionally in our favour — two down, three still going — it was repeatedly feared that a dismal adjustment might have to be made. Whooping cough, measles, diphtheria, pneumonia, to say nothing of lesser complaints such as chicken pox and ringworm, all lay in wait for one or the other of us, and sometimes all of us at once. Cecil came through an attack of scarlet fever only to fall foul of ear infections, just as Daisy had, which in his case led to a double mastoidectomy later on.

Coming as they did one upon the other, these sorts of illnesses created insuperable financial problems for, although most hospital treatment was provided through a hospital insurance stamp scheme, a visit from a doctor was not.

I know now that most parents in Duck Lane endeavoured to pay off these bills by instalments; it was a never-ending debt.

Even childbirth was expensive for, although home-birth was the rule, the fee for a district nurse or a midwife attending a confinement was thirty shillings (£1.50). If a doctor were required, it was two guineas (£2.10). As my mother now reflects, since the lowest of those two fees exceeded half a week's wage for the average workman, it will be readily understood that to receive treatment at home was a ruinous — albeit necessary — expense; more so if the breadwinner were unemployed.

By Easter, 1929, I had suffered most, if not all, of the more common paediatric afflictions and, perhaps due to this and to the ever present squalid environment, I seemed to have built up an immunity or resistance to most things from this time on.

I was never again more than mildly sick; that is with the exception of countless painful abscesses, which flared up intermittently in either ear throughout my young life and, to a lesser extent, plagued me even into manhood.

Now, at just over four and a half, I was old enough to attend school. The Easter holiday ended and one exciting morning I took my place in the noisy convoy of Duck Lane kids. With my sister closest in attendance, I set off for the Church of England school, which lay on the outskirts of the town about half a mile away.

Containing five classrooms, the school was of a typically late Victorian design; similar buildings for the same purpose of strictly local education are scattered all over rural England and appear to vary only in size.

It stood hard by a major highway, the then not-so-busy Petersfield Road, but its rear quarters snuggled into a wild and verdant hillside.

Most of the playground was deeply carpeted with dusty silver sand and the bordering area was a profusion of gorse, fern and whortleberry, interspersed with oak, pine and birch. For many generations this sylvan paradise provided for children at play a wonderful make-believe jungle, ardently inviting kids of all ages to act out the death-defying exploits of their favourite adventure story characters. If you will forgive the pun, in my day it was easily Tarzan who was the most aped.

My first day at school seemed to consist of being eagerly pressed by a lady teacher to play with a little model farm complete with tiny, metal animals. And then for the rest of the day being persuaded not to because I was too noisy with my farmyard impressions. Scholastically it was an inauspicious start, but as time passed I was to become very fond of all aspects of school life: except for two subjects, namely handicraft and gardening, in that order.

I loved Sundays more than ever. Uncle Harry would ask me how I fared at school and I eagerly recounted all that I remembered of the lessons from the preceding week. I was soon to teach him a new hymn, "All things bright and beautiful". He was very pleased about this.

The boxing bouts had become more instructive. My brother was a year-old weakling, and I was repeatedly told by both Father and Uncle Harry that I would have to look out for him as well as myself in the years ahead. Under my uncle's tuition I began to throw straight lefts, followed by right crosses in a highly useful manner. But there was always fun at the end of the lesson, for Uncle Harry still allowed me to knock him over the parapet with the last blow of the contest.

As always, after he had fully recovered, we went off to the Wheatsheaf.

I was aware as I grew that little bit older that Uncle Harry was a very popular person with grown-ups, too. He was quite a comedian and he was no mean entertainer when it came to a comic song. He possessed a loveable nature, and was ever ready to give a helping hand to friend and stranger alike.

Thus there was much concern when the word went round that he was unwell, to be followed soon after with the graver news that he had taken to his bed.

I overheard low voices discussing the merits of strange things like steam kettles and linseed poultices, and I noticed people were inclined to talk about him in whispers. Then came the news that he had been admitted to hospital suffering from pneumonia and pleurisy. In spite of my few years I had been ill many times and I had seen sickness in others many times, but we all got better after a while. Why then was everybody so glum, and even secretive?

It was nine years' old Daisy who broke the news to me. I was leaning against the fireguard in our front room gazing into the red-hot coals when she appeared beside me and blurted out between her sobs that Uncle Harry was dead. He was forty-two.

My father was inconsolable, for he and his brother had been very close. It was the first and last time I ever saw him cry.

I did not cry at all simply because I did not understand. Death was incomprehensible to my tiny mind. In a bewildered imagination I saw it as a state of perpetual illness and failed to understand why Uncle Harry could not recover; it was not like him to give up so easily and to lie in bed all the time.

Because I shed no tears Daisy, misunderstanding my lack of emotion, accused me almost hysterically of never having loved Uncle Harry, and that I was entirely heartless was plain to see.

There might well have been a grain of truth in this for, although we are loved from the moment of birth, I doubt that we are capable of loving until we are a little more matured than I was at that time.

If I were too young to have really loved Uncle Harry then, I have truly loved the memory of him.

CHAPTER
FOUR

Early Lessons

Poor we were, but we never went hungry. The meat, never of the best cut, was served mostly in puddings or stews. Bacon pudding was a great favourite. We spread margarine upon our bread instead of expensive butter — there was a distinct difference in price as well as in taste in those days — and a considerable amount of water was the basis for a milk pudding. But there was always an abundance of fresh vegetables.

Almost all the married men of the working-class community residing in the town paid a nominal annual rent for a parish allotment. For the many it was an economic necessity; for the few it simply eased the weekly shopping budget; for the whole it was a pleasant, productive hobby.

Television had not yet arrived and wireless sets were expensive. The garden, besides being a popular topic of conversation, was also a meeting place where one could exchange idle gossip. And, hidden in the large wooden toolboxes, which served a dual purpose as garden seats, were the bottles of homemade wine.

My father rented an allotment, which lay about a quarter of a mile away in the parish field at June Lane, a lovely walk, which stemmed off into the countryside, opposite the North Street end of Duck Lane.

It is incidental to relate that June Lane ended at its junction with the main highway at a point just above our school, on the opposite side of the road. For our journey to school and back we had, therefore, the choice of two routes, differing very little in distance.

Although I spent a lot of out-of-school hours with my father at the allotment, I was usually there under duress. A bonfire might stimulate my interest, but Father freely acknowledged that the garden seemed to offer very small appeal to me. And I knew, even as a toddler, that I was taken there primarily to get me out and from under my mother's feet. "Gives the missus a break," Father would say.

Almost every allotment had a small plot set aside for the purpose of growing flowers. There was, of course, a minority of less aesthetically minded who threw scorn upon the very idea. "Can't eat ruddy flowers."

One warm summer — I was approaching my fifth birthday — my father achieved a monumental success in the field of arum lilies or, to be more precise, in a row of arum lilies.

The parish field at June Lane covered a big area; it contained dozens of allotments, but men walked over from the most distant points just to view Father's lilies. They were apparently magnificent specimens, and he was rightly proud of them. To me, they were simply big flowers. Nevertheless, I thought my mother might like to see them and, since she seldom visited the garden, there seemed to be but one course to take.

One morning, when my father was fortunate enough to be temporarily employed at a building site, I took a friend with me, younger than I, and went along to the allotments. There we broke off every lily at ground level and carried them, as two huge bouquets, home to Mother. Was there ever a kind and thoughtful deed, which brought forth such an adverse reaction?

My young pal and I were standing on the step of our front door, each holding a great bunch of prize arum lilies. My mother was looking down at us, her face horror stricken. "Oh, my God. Whatever will your father say?"

Neighbours appeared on all sides, echoing in the main and in a like manner her very words.

She berated me, I thought, unmercifully, but she gave me an early tea that afternoon before Father arrived home for she knew that part of my punishment would include being sent to bed without partaking of tea or supper. Later as I lay in bed reflecting upon the monstrous injustices dealt out by grown-ups, I found myself thinking that Mother was not too bad, and I felt quite grateful for the quick feed she had provided just before he came home. Perhaps secretly she even appreciated our floral tribute.

Strangely enough, at no time were we children spanked by our father, yet his word was obeyed without question or hesitation. I think it was his sheer constancy that created such discipline. Whatever the sentence there would be no remission. Early to bed without tea or supper (on this occasion, that's what he thought!), no fishing on Saturday, or no ramble on

Sunday, meant just that. A thick ear could never have commanded more respect.

For this latest transgression he had thrown the book at me, and it was some little while before life resumed its pleasurable normality.

Fishing was one of my early delights, although I fast lost this interest, even as a boy. But the ban at that time was the hardest one to bear. It was another source of food and Father took advantage of it. I was never under duress on a riverbank with Father. I loved fishing then.

The river Rother, which curves around the northern edge of Midhurst, was teeming with fleshy nutriment. There were, of course, certain restrictions. Fishing rights were granted to a specific number of rods, presumably by the Lord Of The Manor's piscatorial representative. These rights were held by a small coterie of mainly professional people, which boasted a wide range of sophisticated equipment. I remember as a youngster laboriously reading the notice boards, which were spaced along the riverbank prohibiting unauthorised fishing. I think eel fishing was permitted to a wider public, but if perchance any other fish adhered to the hook, such as a succulent looking trout, I suppose we were expected to throw it back. We never did.

My father did not aspire in any way to gain recognition as an angler, nor did he fish purely in the interest of sport. He fished principally for food and he fished without a rod. He was an accomplished eel catcher and he used lay-lines, maybe a dozen or more at a time. A lay-line consisted of a length of twine attached at one end to a wooden peg about seven or eight inches long, while the other end first passed through a cork, then a small lead weight, and ended tied firmly to a hook. Common earthworms were used as bait.

A line was cast wherever it was deemed favourable; this was my father's forte, his foresight regarding the movements of eels was remarkable. The wooden peg was thrust deep into the damp earth of the riverbank, preferably close to the waterline, in an endeavour to minimise the risk of detection. Most of Father's lines were placed in the shadows of overhanging trees for the very same reason. And, always, lines were laid overnight, even after a good day's catch.

By this method we were able to fish several stretches of the river at one time, and I have many happy memories of running at Father's side as he strolled at regular intervals throughout the day from one set of line to another.

Wherever there was a catch he used to quickly pull in the line, detach the hook from the fish and slipping the poor creature into the sack that he always carried with him, and which also contained an assortment of our totally unsophisticated equipment. He then swiftly threaded a fresh bait onto the hook and reset the line. There was one snag to this itinerant method of fishing: while we were elsewhere, a sharp-eyed rogue might easily pull in a line and help himself to our fish.

Our record haul was made on a cloudy, sultry Saturday. I had just celebrated my fifth birthday and, to prove to everyone that I was nearly a grown-up, I insisted that I was old enough to accompany my father from the dawn's first light. We found four eels caught by overnight lines and, despite the intervention of rain and thunder, we continued to patrol our fishing grounds until late afternoon.

Once during the morning it rained so heavily we were forced to seek shelter in the confines of a small construction made of little more than long, arched sheets of corrugated iron over a concrete floor. An appalling stench filled the air. Father explained, this was where the dead bodies of horses, cows, and other unfortunate farm animals, most of whom were mortally injured by way of accident, were brought to be cut up before being consumed by the pack of noisy and ravenous foxhounds that lived in the nearby kennels.

It would seem that small quantities of decaying flesh were held back at times for this was the place many local anglers depended upon for maggots.

The floor of the building looked fairly well scrubbed and the interior as a whole seemed quite clean. I think the revolting smell arose from the soak away system, part of which found its way down a narrow gully to the river, giving our prey no doubt a variety of diet.

At the time we were forced to shelter in this establishment we were both feeling hungry, but, although we carried sandwiches in our pockets, a long spell elapsed after leaving the place before either of us felt disposed to eat.

The end of the day saw us triumphantly plodding home with a total haul of four trout and thirteen eels. Because we had no means of refrigeration, the amount surplus to our requirements was soon distributed among our grateful neighbours. Needless to say the smell of fried fish pervaded all quarters of Duck Lane at breakfast time on Sunday.

On Saturday evening mother had a bit of a fright. It was before we had distributed any of the eels and one of them, deceptively well alive, escaped over the edge of the sink where the whole catch had been placed to be washed off under a running tap.

Father was somewhere outside at the time and mother, who never touched eels until Father had skinned and cut them up ready for the frying-pan, was standing near the sink when it happened. She ever regarded them as being too snake-like to invite her approbation, so that her extreme consternation at the sight of a large eel wriggling about the scullery floor might well be imagined.

Finding no suitable refuge in the scullery the eel moved into the front room where, despite my valiant attempts diving over and under the furniture, it proved too elusive for me to catch. Eventually mother's yells brought my father into the house. He soon caught and despatched the poor creature.

Although presumably we did not break a law of the land by fishing for eels, the local angling fraternity frowned most severely upon us, and others like us. There were many veiled threats as well as some not so abstruse.

My father was once warned by an irate angler, who was also locally an influential person, that if he continued to catch eels along a certain stretch of water he could expect to remain unemployed.

Father was not intimidated; merely assuming a lower profile he carried on. In fact to fish with lay-lines under such conditions provided an added excitement; it was akin to poaching.

To be fair the anglers presented points of view that were not without at least a modicum of truth and I doubt that any one of them could seriously imagine an eel-catcher pulling in his lines so that he would not inadvertently hook a trout seen swimming in a near vicinity. Their unanimous assertion was, therefore, that we infringed the rights bestowed upon them. They also accused us of cruelty. A fish, they argued, might remain hooked on an unattended line for an incalculable length of time, in the end perhaps dying miserably from starvation.

If this were not purely hypothetical and proof had been forthcoming to substantiate such an incident, I am positive to this day that my father would not have stood among the guilty. In any case an argument along those lines was always undermined by the fact that fishing in any manner is not the most merciful of pastimes.

But at that time all this moralizing was way above my comprehension. I listened to men heatedly debating and, because I understood so little, I felt nothing: not even sorry for the poor fish. But I did feel anger when on occasions our lay-lines were deliberately cut loose with the peg left in position to remind us perhaps of our folly.

Most of the eel-catchers blamed the anglers for this nefarious practice and, surprisingly enough, many a finger of suspicion was pointed directly at our local incumbent, the Rev. F. Tatchell. I saw nothing to confirm such accusations, but my young mind registered the hearsay of grown-ups. And, after all, I had seen him angling. In consequence of this I allowed myself to harbour lively suspicions and, from a safe distance, whenever the opportunity arose, I kept a close watch upon the riverside activities of the prime suspect.

It was not the result of my observations, they were negative anyway, which influenced my abominable transgression included in the following anecdote, but if the reverend gentleman had been guilty of cutting our lay-lines then, without intent, I was to serve out retribution astonishingly close to what might have been called poetic justice.

CHAPTER
FIVE

The Vicar's Garden

In the chronicles of Midhurst the Rev. F. Tatchell deserves a prominent place. A man of independent means, he was able to take leave of his parish, sometimes for long spells, indulging in his love of globetrotting. When at home he enjoyed a drink at the local club, was well respected by the less secular of his flock, and was ever ready to help a worthy cause. He was benefactor to any passing tramp who had only to knock upon his door to qualify for one pair of new boots annually, and throughout the parish his generosity was in evidence. Entirely under his auspices many attractive sites in and around the town were endowed with comfortable wooden benches, and it was as a result of his adopted responsibility that funds were available whenever such a place was in need of manpower to protect its charms against the encroachments of nature.

To say the least he was a man of whimsical ideas. On more than one occasion he had been seen riding out of town on horseback at a very early hour of the morning; not in itself an odd event, but the purpose sometimes was. Way out in the country where he would most likely go unrecognised he might seek out a lonely and humble cottage whereupon, having gained entry by recounting a plausible tale of woe, his next move was to beg for a breakfast.

It would seem that he often ate the meal with great relish, but rarely with much show of gratitude. Having finished, without more ado, it was his custom to mount up and ride off with barely a grunt of farewell. But left under a plate or saucer was always a sizeable remuneration. In one instance as much as half a guinea (52½p) was discovered by one fortunate woman: a sum that was then more than a day's pay for many.

The vicarage was in North Street. It possessed a pretty garden, about the size of a couple of tennis courts, concealed at one corner by the house itself and for the remainder of its perimeter by fairly high walls. Known as the Vicar's Garden this partly exotic botanical display was open to all. Indeed upon the door leading in from the main street was a sign inviting one to "Enter and to Rest Awhile".

The English flora was liberally interspersed with plants of a more extraneous nature — some were from tropical climes — and all of this was contained in irregular plots upon a lawn also chequered with little paving slabs, placed after the fashion of stepping stones, to take the main weight of pedestrian traffic. And should a breeze, however gentle, reach into the garden, a wonderful sound of tintinnabulation was produced by a string of little bells brought from far away Japan. There was an ornamental pond where water lilies curtsied at the passing of a fish, and there were two large and shady summerhouses containing furniture, tapestries and rugs from all quarters of the world. Either provided a cool retreat where one might sit amid bric-a-brac of all designs and purpose, mostly alien to the English eye. One particular piece of furniture, which we kids loved, was a big velvet-covered seat called the "Wishing Chair". It was supposed to function in much the same way as a wishing-well.

The garden door was locked at night and, although by day the grounds could doubtless be observed from within the house, I am amazed that such artistic odds and ends were left unguarded. I can only conclude that a far stronger code of honour existed then than is to be generally found today.

On a fine afternoon the garden would be occupied mostly by children making up little family groups and supervised by the mother or the eldest member of the family. Each group usually possessed a picnic basket of some sort, which contained no more than the average teatime fare, but which indisputably tasted so much nicer under these conditions. I think perhaps there was an unwritten rule, or a mutual understanding among the visitors, never to overcrowd the garden for I never once saw the place uncomfortably populated.

Most mornings the garden was quiet. A few children might play on the lawns or climb the numerous small trees, usually under the watchful eye of older brothers or sisters, but there were many occasions when it was deserted.

It was at such a time that I, almost six, together with my friend, Dick, who was two years younger, decided to explore the Vicar's Garden on our own. The day was warm but windy and the little bells were ringing merrily.

We decided first to investigate the dark interiors of the summerhouses, but we quickly rejected the idea. The sunlight, darting through willow and trembling silver birch, danced upon the furnishings creating shadowy, menacing forms that flitted around the walls appearing and disappearing in a most weird manner. "Too spooky," we agreed.

I remember we rummaged around in a tiny plantation of bamboo, but discovered nothing of riveting interest and then, entirely without premeditation, we came upon the fishpond. We watched the rather large goldfish as they glided elegantly and effortlessly back and forth just beneath the surface of the wind-whipped waters. One after another they disappeared for long moments under the water lily leaves before sliding into view again to repeat, rather boringly we thought, much the same journey in much the same way.

We soon found out that if we struck the surface of the water with out hands the poor fish would dart about in all directions in absolute panic, then they seemed to realise that the water lily leaves afforded them a place of refuge. In minute that had all disappeared beneath this green and restless canopy. Poor misguided fish; they had no chance at all.

Our hunting instincts were roused; where the leaves grew thickest we proceeded to thin them out, tossing the debris all over the place. There was to be no hiding room for those wretched goldfish.

It was Dick who landed the first one and it was, he afterwards declared, entirely accidental. Plunging his hand into the gloomy depths of the pond he scooped up a fish as well as a leaf or two, and in the same movement flung the whole lot into the air from whence the fish landed first upon the sunlit lawn, there to wriggle and gasp its life away. Accidental or not I was not to be outdone by a younger kid and it was only minutes before a second goldfish writhed alongside the first victim.

By the time we had landed a dozen or so our clothing had become saturated and the strong wind, playing upon our damp flesh, had a decidedly chilling effect. The excitement was on the wane and I think I experienced certain misgivings, for without hesitation I decided against taking the catch home. We turned our backs on the ghastly shambles and hurriedly made our way from the garden into North Street.

In this street stood the public hall, a large building, which at the time was in use mainly as a cinema, although other functions did sometimes take place there. Just inside the entrance there was, to the right of the foyer, a small office, which served as an employment exchange. The entrance to the foyer was reached from the street by climbing a wide flight of stone steps. We had to pass it on our way home.

In front of this imposing edifice was a queue of men reaching back some twenty yards. Its tail stretched along the pavement, the centre of it snaked its way up the flight of steps, and its head disappeared into the office just off the foyer.

My father stood in this queue and he saw us. That he had not seen us emerge from the Vicar's Garden was apparent. "Where the devil 'ave you two been?" he asked and before we could answer, "Down that river by the looks of you."

I could not but help notice that Father was the only stern-looking man in the queue. All the other men seemed to be laughing at our bedraggled appearance. "Get off 'ome right now," he said most severely, "I've told you before to keep away from the river unless a grown-up's with you."

We scuttled off to Duck Lane and young Dick, who lived next door to my grandmother, squelched his lonely way up the steps. I learned soon afterwards that he was duly berated by his mother, but as yet only for arriving home in such a wet state.

Upon entering our scullery I saw that Mother was sweating over the sink labouring hard washing clothes. Not a very good moment I thought. In a cunning effort to assuage her I went in off the deep end as it were. A figure of speech well supported by my appearance. I immediately declared that Father had already seen me and had grumbled at me ever so much. Desperately groping for a possible shred of compassion, I told my tale.

"He told me I mustn't go down the river to play ever again. Dick and me both got wet. Dick got wetter than me. We didn't mean to get wet. The long grass was ever so wet by the riverbank. Dad didn't 'alf tell me off."

It had to be that way; the river and the riverside must take full blame. I must not mention the Vicar's Garden. The enormity of our wicked act had by then completely dawned upon me. The possibility of it being discovered and of a charge being laid at my door worried me greatly. I prayed that Dick had said nothing about the Vicar's Garden and that his story allied itself to mine as we had agreed.

That evening I went off to bed feeling fairly optimistic. Father had again admonished me, warning me afresh about the perils of playing by the riverside. Mother had entreated me, throwing in a threat or two for good measure, never again to come home in such a state.

All things considered, the future looked promising. I began to feel that we had not been seen at the fishpond and, so long as young Dick did not let the cat out of the bag, all seemed bright. That last well known expression put a thought in my mind, a thought full of fervent hope: that a hungry cat, or cats, might devour all the remains of the goldfish just as I had seen the cats of Duck Lane eating the scraps of many a fish breakfast. So thinking I fell asleep.

Wishful thinking upon the eve, that is all it was. Came grim reality with the morning. I was wakened by Father who looked dreadfully cross. He stood at the top of the stairs glaring down at me and I had the feeling he might burst with temper at any moment. The veins at his temple appeared very blue and swollen.

But, with commendable restraint, he spoke slowly with a frightening, intense deliberation. "You're goin' to get up now, wash and dress, and at nine o'clock you're goin' on your own to the Vicar's house. You'll knock the front door and wait. Reverend Tatchell will answer the door and he will take you in. I don't know whether or not you'll ever come out again and right now I don't particularly care. The vicar is in a right old temper about you and, for that matter, so am I. You'll tell him the truth about what you got up to yesterday and you'll apologise. No, I don't want you to tell me about Dick; you're a lot older than him. Furthermore, I'll be standin' at the corner watchin' you all the way, so there'll be no avoidin' the issue."

And there was not.

I think during the next hour or so I experienced all that a condemned man must feel as he waits to take that last short walk. It would be far easier if I could die quietly here at home. I wondered if I could hold my breath long enough to achieve this. I wished I had the power to turn myself into a flea or a beetle; their lives, although always in danger from Keating's Power, seemed much safer than mine.

I looked around with great fondness at my humble surroundings; even the smelly old lavatories appeared dear to me. In fact, I thought of seeking refuge in one of them, but I knew Father would find me.

★ ★ ★

Many times I had seen the Rev. F. Tatchell along the riverside, but never at really close quarters. From a distance, to me, he looked a bit ghostly with his very pale features and what might be described as a halo of white hair.

And there was his house, too. The rear of his home, which bordered on the garden, we kids had ever regarded with a certain amount of awe. It was always so silent and eerie and the windows displayed no movements from within. The heavy back door was at all times locked, and we wondered what mysteries lay behind it, or what horrors it might conceal.

Of course all that really existed was a delightfully quiet atmosphere; the rest was made up from those enjoyable figments of imagination so exclusive to children, for how we loved to frighten ourselves. That morning there was absolutely no need for me to attempt to frighten myself; I was about to enter that house. I was standing at the front door of the vicarage. I had knocked once, just one sharp tap. In order to operate the heavy ornamental knocker, which was way above my reach, it had been necessary for me to execute a standing jump, flinging the knocker upwards at the same time with my outstretched hand. Gravity did the rest.

Father had ordered me to do this; knowing the door was thick he realised my puny fist might well beat unheard upon the woodwork. By so doing he anticipated, and closed, a possible last avenue of escape, even if it led to no more than procrastination.

I looked desperately up and down the street, but every hope was forlorn. Father, implacable as ever, remained standing at the turning to Duck Lane just as he said he would. He had no need to stand sentinel for I was quite unable to run away. My little feet seemed glued to the pavement; my legs rigid as though splinted together. No nightmare was ever as bad as this. I was petrified.

The door opened without warning and a hand emerged from the shadows, fastening on to my shoulder very tightly. A voice somewhere above me said, "Come in, boy."

In that one brief moment I bade a silent farewell to all that I loved. And I found, surprisingly enough, my father was still included. Then I was hauled unresisting over the threshold.

Blinking in the dim light of a hallway I was propelled into a lavishly furnished room. My captor sat down on a straight-backed wicker chair and I was made to stand facing him.

He did not look at all like my idea of a ghost, but even so I continued to regard him with horror. I wondered what real live ogres looked like and immediately found myself speculating as to whether they lived in vicarages as well as in castles.

There was no glimmer of tender heartedness in that pale, expressionless face. I watched, mesmerised, as he gazed down at me half expecting a forked tongue rather than words to issue from those tightly pursed lips.

The seconds dragged by. I was certain that I must die before anything else happened for my heart was lodged, almost painfully, just behind my Adam's apple and was thumping away fit to choke me.

The Reverend Tatchell finally spoke, very briefly this time, just enough to prompt me into confessing in a somewhat faltering voice due to my seemingly restricted larynx, to the heinous crimes of which I stood accused. I was then asked to repent and I earnestly expressed my great sorrow without any prompting at all. (I was never so sorry for myself in all my young life!)

Then I cowered before a tirade such as I had never experienced. There were parts of the censure I did not understand, but I asked no questions and I was to remember for a very long time the way in which it was given. Most of it found its mark and before it was ended I was feeling terribly guilty and utterly wretched. The case had been summed up. Fearfully I awaited sentence. I was never noted for crying easily, but I was near to tears right then.

There was an unbearable silence broken at length by the rattle of a motor vehicle passing by in the faraway outside world. My tormentor stood up, his voice still sharp. "Come this way, boy."

I was ushered through the house to the back door. My legs were no longer petrified; they felt more like jelly and they trembled in like manner. The bolts were withdrawn and we stepped into the garden. There, at the scene of the crime, the evidence was grim and incontestable. No hungry cats had been around here. The dead fish and the shrivelled water lily leaves remained strewn around the denuded pond.

I was given the task of clearing up this frightful mess and the Reverend Tatchell watched in silence as I piled all of yesterday's debris into an old incinerator. I carried out this job in a fairly short time, but it was still prolonging my alarming concern for my future — if there were to be one.

Then the most amazing thing happened. My persecutor was looking down at me with the semblance of a smile upon his pallid features. At the same time he pressed a whole half crown piece into my sweaty little hand.

His final comments were more or less as follows: "Ronald," — this was the only time he spoke my name — "You've cleared things up very tidily this morning, but that does not put right what you did yesterday. You may tell your father, however, that you have been honest with me and that I think you were quite brave in coming to see me on your own."

(When I later recounted this to Father, "I'll bet the Vicar didn't know I watched you all the way," was his immediate comment.)

The reverend gentleman had by this time, with one hand resting upon my shoulder, steered me to the gate, which opened into North Street. He gave one last counsel: "You may come to this garden as often as you wish, but never again to do mischief." I was dismissed.

As I ran light-heartedly up the street I took my leave, not of a ghost, not of an ogre, but in my new estimation, a gentleman and a first-class sport. I felt so happy, so relieved, I wanted to sing, laugh and whistle all at the same time. As Father was not to be seen, I did not run straight home. I fancied a celebration was in order for what I truly regarded then as an extension of my life. How does a lone, fairly rich, six years' old boy celebrate? With the help of a sweet shop, of course.

I spent a whole six-pence; in those days such a sum purchased a large amount of sweets. Sucking at a bar of milk chocolate I walked homewards carrying two paper bags full of slab toffee, which the lady in the shop had broken to manageable pieces with her little all-metal hammer. The lady, who knew me well, looked slightly surprised when I handed her the half crown (12½p), but she said nothing, giving a florin piece (10p) in change.

It rested in my trousers pocket. I must hide it in a safe place, for Father might confiscate it, feeling that the Vicar had been much too liberal. Stuffing the bags of toffee well inside my shirt I turned into Duck Lane.

There were some big gates in the wall, which sealed off the backyard of the International Stores. Just inside to the left there stood a huge elderberry tree, tucked neatly away in a quiet corner. It was immediately opposite my front door, but was mostly screened by the high wall. The gates were open; I slipped in and climbed into the tree.

Near the top there was a branch that, at an early stage of its development, had been split lengthways at its base, a deformity that had not restricted its growth. The resulting deep fissure provided a very good hiding place for small valuables. I used it often, for mostly fanciful rather than necessary reasons. Placing the florin piece carefully within I climbed to the ground.

I crossed the lane and went indoors. Mother, all agog, asked me how I had fared at the vicarage and I related a scrupulously accurate story of my encounter with the Rev. F. Tatchell, except for the conclusion. I said, rather vaguely, that the Vicar had paid for the toffee, which I was eating. Mother seemed quite relieved and entirely satisfied with my story, so I soon made off through the back door in search of my pal, young Dick.

I found him sitting on the steps below my grandmother's house. He was delighted to see me and I quickly recounted the morning's adventure — leaving out the bit about how scared I was — and then I asked had he given the game away.

His strenuous, even indignant, denial satisfied me and we sat there talking it over, but we could not decide, nor for that matter did we ever discover, just how our guilt had been revealed.

Dick gratefully accepted a bag of broken toffee, but I did not disclose the full amount of money I had received, nor did I divulge that I had more cash in reserve, hidden away for another day, on high in an elderberry tree.

CHAPTER
SIX

Miscellaneous Memories

During this period of my young life I had suffered on several occasions with severe earache. Small abscesses would flare up deep in either ear, sometimes in both, thumping away to the heart's beat for long distressing hours. Years later, comparing experiences with my brother who was also to endure this same trouble, we were agreed that one could actually hear the pain. It was a veritable crescendo of torment that gradually obliterated all normal sounds. It was a lonely world of pulsating torture until that sharper, searing agony, which, suddenly abating, mercifully told the sufferer that the gathering had burst. The warm flow of pus, running freely from the ear, brought instant blessed relief.

For such a contingency an old-fashioned application, one which I will still swear by in the absence of modern drugs, was a bag of hot salt. In my considerable experience it was most effective and very simple to make.

A cloth bag, about four inches square, was filled with a quantity of table salt. This was then heated to a bearable degree and held to the ear. The warmth alleviated the intense pain to a fair extent and most certainly brought the abscess to a head in a much shorter time. Our local doctors seemed to approve of this palliative and, if there were any unspoken doubts as to its efficacy, it had to be reasoned that it could do no harm. I only know that, with the first pangs of earache, I cried out for a hot salt bag and Mother quickly obliged.

Alas, the trouble became persistent and eventually an operation was advised; it was thought that a minor piece of surgery upon my throat might clear up the source of infection. A straightforward tonsillectomy, together with the removal of the adenoids, was subsequently carried out at the local Cottage Hospital. I was not detained there for long and it was not a particularly interesting sojourn. The worse part of it all was the sickening smell of the chloroform, an anaesthetic with a truly evil odour. Anything remotely like it I find repulsive to this day. Small as I was then I put up a tremendous struggle as the chloroform-steeped mask — it looked like a very large tea strainer — was forced upon my face.

The after-effect of this loathsome anaesthetic was nearly as bad as the initial application, for one always regained consciousness (it seemed to me in this and subsequent operations) in dire need of a kidney-shaped basin in which to painfully vomit. Strangely I do not recall the use of anaesthetic or of being sick at the time of my hernia repair. I have often wondered about this, for such treatment must surely have produced the most vivid of recollections and I remember only the stitches being removed.

The immediate result of this present operation, so far as I was concerned, was a sore throat, but since this was soothed with nice fruit flavoured drinks and dollops of ice cream, things were looking good I thought.

The operation seemed for a while to be successful in correcting my middle ear disorders. But only for a while.

Father, meanwhile, had found work at a stone quarry, about a couple of miles away in the village of Easebourne. My spell of convalescence had ended and I was then attending school, but on a Saturday, when Father worked in the morning only, I would get up early and go with him to the quarry.

As I recall, a dozen or so men were employed there, most of them wielding heavy hammers and iron bars. Upon reflection, balls and chains and arrowed suits would have complemented such surroundings.

It was late autumn, the weather cool, but I remember how the sweat poured down the faces of the workmen, and how their shirts turned a darker hue from perspiration soaking through as they toiled away with the sledgehammers, excavating huge stones and then reducing them to a required size.

I recall a one-armed man called Harry who, despite his disability, was able to swing a huge hammer with one arm as effectively as any man with two. He told me he had left his other arm somewhere in France under a heap of mud.

It was very hard work. By the end of the day it must have been cruel, but I now realise, remembering the widespread poverty, not one man there would have changed his lot for unemployment.

We progress to Christmas and, poor though we are, we enjoyed it.

Poverty, when not actually knocking upon the door, was always in close proximity, but our parents somehow were able to give us ever a wonderful time at Christmas. How they did so is not quite a mystery; it was brought about by a combination of incredible thrift and self-discipline.

In those days almost every shop ran a Christmas club. A customer would pay in perhaps six pence a week or even less, and at around mid-December would draw goods to the value of the amount saved. There were also Slate Clubs — usually formed in public houses — which, besides helping one to save for Christmas, paid a small weekly sum for a limited period to any member who happened to fall sick, rendering him or her incapable of earning a living. Many clubs made stringent rules regarding the behaviour of a sick member. For example, a person drawing benefit must not be seen outside of home after a stated hour in the evening. The actual hour varied with the time of year, there being a slight extension during summer months. It is difficult to understand the reason for a curfew being imposed upon a person suffering from perhaps a broken arm, but there were no exceptions to the rule. Whatever amount was in the kitty at the end of a year was shared equally among all members just before Christmas.

My mother, too, ran a savings club, which was made up of members of the family and quite a number of our neighbours at Duck Lane. Some deposited as little as three pence a week, but it all counted when the festive season arrived. I remember the strong metal box in which the money was held, and how it was always kept locked and hidden away in the cupboard by the fireplace in the front room. It seemed to me that everyone was so determined to celebrate at least once a year.

In another quarter of our front room stood a worn, but workable, wind-up gramophone complete with a big tin horn. It was worn, because, like everything else in the house, it was second-hand at least. It was not played a great deal, I suppose due to a shortage of records, but every Christmas morning before breakfast, when the excitement of emptying our pillowcases of toys and things was still upon us, my father would play a few carols. He always opened with his favourite, "Hark the Herald Angels Sing", and he always played it more than once.

To this day, when I hear that carol, I relive those magic mornings in that so very humble home and I remember with wonder and gratitude how my parents provided such lovely times for us, the kids, on Christmas Day, in spite of the mostly all the year round adverse conditions.

Soon after entering the New Year the Christmas tree was returned to the June Lane allotment, where it was replanted in its usual corner. Over the years this sturdy little tree became a regular visitor to our home, albeit only once a year and then only for the duration of a fortnight or so. That it did not resent this treatment was evident for it grew slowly yet surely bigger and was still to be with us after I passed out of my teens.

Most youngsters like a game of football, but I think I had more than an average predilection for the game. The sound of an old tennis ball, new ones were not seen in Duck Lane, or perhaps an old beach-ball sometimes stuffed with rag, being kicked around the drying ground would compel me to drop everything and rush to the scene of action. For me only two things governed the length of the game: one was the durability of the ball, the other depended upon whether or not the drying ground was required for its real purpose. Many were the occasions we were unceremoniously chased off by a justifiably irate laundress.

When anyone was fortunate enough to produce a real football it was never played with in or around the lane. There were too many sharp projections in those old walls, including scores of rusty nails. It was then that the green outskirts of Midhurst beckoned imperatively. A field of grass and a couple of jackets or pullovers to serve as goalposts, an imaginary capacity crowd, and what feats we would perform in the interest of club or country!

In reality, because we played mostly on pasture land, any spectators we might attract consisted mainly of mildly inquisitive cows, always chewing lugubriously at the one end, while from time to time unconcernedly depositing cowpats at the other. Each one of us would inevitably at some stage of the game come into close and undesirable contact with such a deposit, much to the amusement of the others. "Cor, you've been really fouled!" was the trite, yet always laughed at, exclamation.

Although our immediate home surroundings were no better than those of children living in city slums, we did have that one great advantage: our countryside was not a million miles away.

As we of an age group left our nursery years behind we began to play at Cowboys and Indians, or perhaps gave our first spirited performances in our early interpretations of the goodies and baddies of medieval Sherwood Forest. Whatever the whim, we were always aware that these games, like football, could only be properly played outside the crumbling confines of Duck Lane, and around Midhurst could be found the backcloth for any outdoor drama.

"Cowdray Ruins" provided the remains of a large fortified mansion, burnt down in 1973. Several English monarchs had visited this once magnificent house and there is to this day enough stonework standing to give a good outline of what it must have looked like before the fire. A lady custodian lived nearby in a little round house. We kids told each other that this was where the heads were chopped off, but in actual fact it was the conduit tower once belonging to the mansion. The conversion made a unique dwelling.

There were numerous occasions when we blighted the life of this poor custodian. We were not permitted to play in the "Ruins", but such a ban merely created a greater attraction. Many were the times that we enjoyed being chased away.

Close by high upon a hill overlooking the river we sometimes scampered over the shallow, stone-built outline of a much earlier domicile: this time a real castle. Only the foundations remained, but these had been recently raised a couple of feet or so to produce a low wall depicting the plan of the ground floor. The whole area was known as St Anne's Hill.

To the south of this hill, not far off, was a wood, which was a complex of yew tree avenues, so we were never short of the traditional material for an English bow. On many a summer day, this place served our purpose as Sherwood Forest. The whole of this superb playground was clustered close to the town; beyond this the countryside was limitless in every respect.

I had by this time lost a great deal of interest in my blue pedal-car, although whenever my brother was feeling up to it I pushed him up and down the lane, teaching him to steer in readiness for the day he would become owner-driver. I had been forced to retire from driving because my legs had outgrown the interior; my kneecaps struck the dashboard all too often.

★　★　★

Before the arrival of spring my father was to be off work again, this time with a badly infected hand. The callused skin of his right hand had been in some way perforated and had resulted in a deep-rooted infection. Despite the alleviatory effect of laudanum there is no doubt he endured more pain from this condition than with anything he had experienced, including the shrapnel wounds and subsequent aggravations.

First the hand became hideously enlarged and then the arm began to swell; remember there were no antibiotics to be had. Kaolin poultice was tried with no success. It would have to be lanced by a doctor, which meant, I suppose, one more bill to pay. Mother regarded this as inevitable and faced up to it, but Father stubbornly delayed this move in the desperate hope that the inflammation would draw to a head and burst of its own accord.

The final twenty-four hours of agony saw him without respite or sleep. In my mind's eye I see him now, pacing up and down the front room, ashen faced and racked with pain.

It was mid-morning when Nan came in. She took everything in at a glance. "Jack, you're bloody stupid. You'll lose your arm and even more if you don't get to a doctor." I think Father was on the point of giving in anyway. Nan's blunt appraisal merely hastened his decision.

The doctor's knife did the job and it was nice to see Father after a day or two looking well again. His hand though remained swathed in a bandage for a week or so and then he had to wait for the skin to harden before he was able to resume working. His employer was under no liability to pay him sick benefit and did not. So it was that, after a promising start, a financial setback arrived early this year.

A little later, the second of July to be precise, something else arrived. This time, unseen by me, a nurse delivered a baby girl to our house. It came as a big surprise to me, but it was not half so exciting as my brother's arrival had been, chiefly because I was out playing at the time on Nan's express orders. Having run all the way home from school, hungry as usual, I found her sitting in our front room. She delegated for Mother and gave me, and a couple of mates who waited at the door for me to go back out to play, a large hunk of bread pudding each.

"Your mum isn't very well," she explained, "I want you to go off to the common to play and you needn't hurry back." The common was much farther away than our usual after school haunts, but without giving it a lot of thought we complied with her command.

When we returned in the early evening I was taken upstairs by Nan and introduced to my younger sister. I was not particularly thrilled, for I was not much taken by girls, not then at any rate.

Commenting on the fact that my mother always seemed to be in bed when the babies were delivered, Nan explained that all mothers stayed in bed in order to keep the babies warm until they grew just a little bit older.

CHAPTER
SEVEN

Carshalton

Statutory holidays with pay had yet to be introduced, therefore my father's circumstances, like those of a million more, ensured that my school day memories would evoke no reminiscences of holidays, home or away, spent together as a family. But I do remember a couple of long weekends, probably including Bank Holidays, spent all together at William Street, Carshalton: a rapidly growing suburb of south London. This was the well-remembered address of my great-aunt Fanny. She was sister to Nan and was in every respect a truly great aunt, with or without the hyphen. These occasions no doubt followed a rare period of full employment for Father.

Aunt Fan, and most people called her Aunt, was a widow with two grown-up daughters: Nancy was married and lived only a short distance away; the one still living at home was Nellie.

Young girls of the neighbourhood, bringing over the years an assortment of broken hearts, empty hearts and even hearts that overflowed with happiness, for some needed to share joy as much as sorrow, would eagerly call upon Aunt Fan. She was to them the fount of wisdom, of understanding and of sympathy. Many a suitor, too, benefited from her advice, seeking it with no embarrassment, for she was so easy to approach.

I often heard her referred to as The Nurse of William Street. That she had received no official training meant little to those who bestowed this appellation upon her. She simply and instinctively played the role of nurse to all who needed help. But she specialised in mending hearts and minds and it was for this she was best known and loved. She catered also for children, for they, too, would run to their "Aunt Fan" in times of woe, knowing that besides words of comfort they might well receive a sweet or two. Her door was ever open and she even had the "Rainbow", a weekly comic, delivered solely for the amusement of any child who might call upon her. I remember she used to go out to work several times a week, domestic cleaning mainly, but like my Nan she was pretty poor.

She was a most endearing character and she thought the world of me. Small wonder that I was to holiday there, travelling on my own, at least once a year for the remainder of my boyhood. Nearly a month short of my seventh birthday, I was about to embark upon my first solo journey. I had been looking forward to it so very much for weeks.

The train fare was four shillings and two pence return; this was half fare, which converted to today's currency is just over twenty pence. I had contributed towards this large amount by doing a variety of odd jobs, and by literally picking up a few handfuls of coppers during Goodwood Week; this I will explain later for it deserves a full account. It is suffice to say that because of that particular week I had, tucked away upon my person in one of Mother's old purses, a surplus of cash, about two shillings I think, to spend as pocket money.

Mother escorted me to Midhurst railway station where she purchased my ticket and, because the train was already at the platform, immediately placed me in the care of the guard in whose van I was to journey. He was a very likeable man and no doubt reliable, but, since I would travel only part of the way with him, a label was fixed in the lapel of my jacket stating my destination. That I might be mislaid or suffer from amnesia had to be taken into account I suppose, but I remember feeling quite indignant about being labelled when I could quote Aunt Fan's address easily. I could even write it, too!

The guard blew his whistle, shook his flag and jumped aboard, slamming the door behind him. We both waved to Mother through the rear window as the train pulled slowly away. Although we entered a tunnel about a hundred yards or so from the station I could still see Mother waving to us from the platform. It was a bit like looking through the wrong end of a telescope. She began to fade in the grey swirls of smoke and steam and then suddenly, because of a sharp curve in the tunnel, she was gone and all was dark.

Soon I could see the sides of the tunnel flashing past at what seemed a great speed as we steamed towards the sunny outside world. Out of the tunnel, under a bridge, then high above the surrounding countryside we sped along an embankment. I was really on my way; the weeks of dreaming transposed to reality.

I felt a little sorry for the guard who seemed very calm: almost bored I thought. It was evident he was not enjoying the trip half as much as I, and I was astonished on one occasion to see him stifle a long, long yawn. It was to take me a few more years to understand that to do a thing like this almost daily was totally different from doing it for the first time in one's life.

The wonder of that journey will be with me forever. The rhythmic clickety-clack, clickety-clack, clickety-clack heralded the approach of lands unknown as the wheels spun over the rails. Seen from the rear window they seemed to flow like an endless conveyor belt from somewhere beneath us, swiftly converging to a single strip of silver until lost to sight in the distant, receding landscape.

We steamed on through the countryside of Selham, Petworth and Fittleworth, stopping at each of these places to take on and put off all sorts of luggage, and, I suppose, passengers. But I was too concerned with the guard's van and its function to be interested in people.

Upon arriving at Pulborough I experienced a brief moment of sadness: I was parted from both my nice guard and my little train, which for the first time I noticed consisted of only two carriages. I noted the engine was not very big, too, for I was able to compare it to one that was standing at another platform with seven or eight carriages strung behind it. This was not my train and I watched, fascinated, as it pulled away on the next stage of its journey.

In the care of a porter, a surly-looking man with a large moustache, I walked to one end of a very long platform where, amidst a heap of mailbags and sundry items of luggage, I awaited the arrival of another train. This time it was a big engine pulling lots of carriages. One by one they drifted by as the engine slowed to a halt. I thought the train might be too long for the platform and was accordingly worried, but the guard's van stopped right in front of me. The guard, who moved about so quickly I could scarce describe him, promptly placed me in the compartment next to his van; not quite so exciting, but I was still thoroughly enjoying myself.

I changed trains again at Dorking, and then at Sutton, where I boarded an electric train for the last short lap to Carshalton. From then on I travelled in a public compartment. But it was still good fun.

At Carshalton I was met by Aunt Fan and a couple of lads of my own age with whom I was to strike up a close friendship that flourished fully, for at least once a year, throughout the remainder of our schooldays. We were to call ourselves The Three Musketeers of William Street, but we retained our own names, Georgie, Billy and Ron.

Billy lived next door to Aunt Fan, Georgie a few doors away, and throughout all of my holidays at Carshalton we spent most of the days together. During the summer I seldom stayed there for less than a month.

We earned money together, too, useful amounts of pocket money, by shopping for anyone who cared to ask for our service. We used to take the shopping lists all the way to Sutton, about a mile and a half away, where there were bigger and cheaper shops. Piling the merchandise into a converted kiddy-cart, designed and made ourselves, we returned to William Street making a door-to-door delivery of our purchases. We charged each customer two pence, irrespective of the amount of freight required. Sometimes, if we had made a purchase at a greatly reduced price, we received a copper or two as a bonus.

With these proceeds we visited the numerous cinemas in and around the district, including the Granada at Tooting, where we were enthralled by the Mighty Wurlitzer organ, which at set times appeared in front of the stage rising mystically from beneath the floor. Other cinemas had similar organs, but this one was the biggest and certainly the most famous in our district.

We had also to provide money for the tram fares on these excursions (later to be replaced by trolley buses) and we seldom went without a bar of chocolate or an ice cream or two. We did not work every day; our financial needs left us plenty of time for play, but if we planned a treat for ourselves we were prepared to work for it.

★　★　★

73

Aunt Fan was one of my many relatives in the Carshalton area, and over the years I was lucky enough to be taken by uncles, aunts and older cousins to all sorts of interesting places in and around London.

Mitcham Fair, an annual event, brought together the biggest assembly of funfairs I have ever seen. It was rumoured to be the largest in the world. I was fortunate in being able to go there at least once every year during the short time that this huge fair remained amalgamated.

I was taken to see the great Arsenal team of the early 1930s. No one at my school had seen James, Bastin and Hapgood, to name but three of the stars, except perhaps on the cinema newsreels or the obverse side of a cigarette card. I felt very smug about this, even superior.

During my first holiday at Carshalton I was taken on a visit to an aunt and uncle who lived near the Old Kent Road in London. In this unsavoury area I was introduced to a kind of poverty that did not exist back home in Duck Lane. I saw little kids, barefoot and dressed in ragged, dirty clothes, scavenging from a filthy dustbin at the rear of a dingy café. And it looked as though those poor kids needed all they might find.

In this vicinity was a small shop in which I purchased a toy sword complete with scabbard and belt. An aunt had given me the money by way of a present, for it was only a day or so from my seventh birthday.

Before leaving the shop I buckled the belt around my waist and with my trusty sword at my side I stepped proudly into the street. In an instant the sword and belt were ripped from my person and a little fellow about my age was haring up the road bearing away my newly bought gift. I gave chase and easily caught up with him. The road was suddenly full of children, some jeering at me, some cheering at me. Heartened a little by the latter, for I was in alien territory, I proceeded to teach the thief a lesson, remembering all that Uncle Harry had taught me.

The boy relinquished his hold upon the sword and tried to defend himself, but he knew nothing about the noble art and, although I was still angry — I could see that he had broken the belt if nothing more — I was glad when he turned away and ran for it.

He was so thin it had been like hitting at a skeleton and my knuckles were feeling bruised and painful. Over the years I regret ever having given chase to that unfortunate, hungry-looking creature. He had been without shoes and, although my sword would not have compensated for that, it might well have projected one tiny bright spot upon the not so rich tapestry of his dark and squalid life.

Being reminded of skeletons, I can boast of having danced with a real human one on a number of occasions in my young life.

One of Aunt Fan's jobs was as part-time cleaner of a hall which was used for such functions as whist drives, the occasional dance, and regularly once a week provided a meeting place for medical students; the nature or name of this fraternity I never knew.

It was the first time I had been to this place with Aunt Fan and, as she began her chores in the main hall, I prowled around exploring. In a small room used chiefly for making tea and other refreshments I soon discovered a peculiar looking carriage. It was made up of two pairs of wheels, of rather large diameter, supporting a narrow platform upon which rested a long wooden box with a hinged lid.

I thought it would be rather fun to push this wheeled object around the big hall. It did not occur to me that I might get in the way of Aunt Fan. I moved it no more than a yard when the nearside front wheel fell off. The platform tilted just enough to cause the box to crash to the ground on its side. In a vain endeavour to prevent this I, too, fell to the floor, landing on my side, facing the box at exactly the moment the lid dropped open, narrowly missing me. In that split second I very nearly died of fright. It was the first time I had ever come eye-to-eye, or socket-to-socket, with a real — no, not live — dead skeleton!

Looking back I think Aunt Fan handled the situation very wisely. Hearing the crash she hurried into the little room and at once seeing that I was unhurt, albeit scared nearly to death, she laughed and picked me up. She then dragged the skeleton to its feet and backing into the main hall she began to waltz around the room with it. I could see then that the bones were wired together.

"There you are. It's quite harmless. It won't hurt you. Come on, you have a go. Come on, give it a dance."

76

And I did. After that whenever we went to the hall I always played around with it; in fact I grew quite fond of it. Aunt Fan told me that it was the mortal remains of a full grown male. Since I was not quite seven when I first made its acquaintance that would explain why, even without shoes on its feet and hair on its head, it was so much taller than I when it was propped upright.

Aunt Fan always made me laugh by saying things like, "Get your old pal out of his box. I'll wager he's bored to death in there." Or, "No wonder he's a bit stiff, he doesn't get enough exercise."

Aunt Fan was unable to tell me anything about his origin and I found myself regretting that I knew so little about my silent playmate. To this day I wonder just who he was.

Another interesting place was Croydon Airport. Georgie, Billy and I visited it together many times. In our early years we reached it by tram, superseded as on all the routes by the far less noisy trolley bus. We often spent a whole day on the flat roof of the Airport Terminus, which was open to the public and gave an unrestricted view of all movements in and around the aerodrome. That was, in our case, if we behaved ourselves and were not chased off by an irate official.

Mischief lurks alert in the heart of a healthy boy and we proved no exceptions. Our favourite venial transgression began with filling our pockets with "hundreds and thousands", a confection, which resembled a tiny ball bearing. I doubt that a hundred of them would constitute an average mouthful, and they were very cheap to buy.

Late in the day, when we were tired of watching the planes and, with the devil at our shoulder, we leaned over the parapet, three or four stories high, waiting impatiently for a worthwhile number of people to congregate immediately beneath us. On more than one occasion I remember seeing men with microphones and cameras among the throng. We liked this set-up best of all; it told us there was at least one celebrity or, as we say today, a VIP somewhere down below.

"Ready, steady, go," was the command that precipitated a miniature hailstorm. Handfuls of "hundreds and thousands" fell upon the milling crowd creating, from our point of view, hilarious scenes of confusion and consternation.

That we dared not take a bow or dwell upon our act goes without saying. We would duck back below the parapet and appear quite innocent-looking at a position that did not indicate our involvement.

If we were detected our route of departure lay in the fire escape stairway, which ran down the outside of the building. Our passage down this and thence to the road outside could be calculated in seconds rather than minutes. Safely aboard a tram or trolley bus, we would chuckle all the way to Carshalton.

There were, however, long spells when we musketeers behaved impeccably, usually at the promise of a red-letter day. One such occasion was the prospect of a trip to London Zoo in the care of Billy's mother. How we looked forward to that.

Most of the preceding time found us canvassing hard for extra errands and all kinds of odd jobs. We aimed to be solvent when the great day arrived, and we were.

The morning dawned with a low mist indicating fine weather. In high spirits we set out for the railway station where we boarded a London-bound train. We delighted in the Underground journey from Victoria to Regent's Park and, as we emerged from the well-lit bowels of the earth, the sun broke through the fading mist and London Zoo was bathed in its warm and brilliant light.

The reptile house was our first objective and we spent a long time there — in my case most certainly — paradoxically fascinated by repugnance. It was quite warm inside the building, but by imagining ourselves to be on the other side of the glass panels that front many of the compartments, we enjoyed many a shiver before we strolled out into the really hot summer sunshine.

Meandering through the grounds of the Zoo, Billy and Georgie, and even Billy's mother, fairly bubbled with enthusiasm, babbling away excitedly at each and every observation. I was growing more and more silent. My last effort at enjoyment was made upon the back of an elephant. When the ride was over I slithered slowly down the beast's huge shoulder and in that moment, unable to pretend or ignore it any longer, I gave myself up to the misery and pain of earache.

Billy's mother took me along to a First Aid Post, where the well intended probings by an Angel of Mercy succeeded only in making the pain worse, far worse, and in my eyes the said Angel took on the aspect of a devil's disciple. I was glad to leave that place. Sadly, halfway through what was to have been a great day, we all returned to Carshalton.

I will never forget the agony of that journey. The movement of the train, every curve of the rail, every joint of the line, added to the almost unendurable pain that raged deep inside the ear.

Moreover, I will never forget the kind attitudes adopted by both Billy and Georgie. Although my condition had been responsible for spoiling their day, neither resentment nor blame was levelled at me. I received from them on that day, and long afterwards whenever it was referred to, nothing but genuine sympathy. Children are not always so kind.

Once back at William Street, Aunt Fan swiftly prepared and applied the trusty salt-bag remedy and in the early hours of the following day the abscess burst and the pain immediately abated. For a couple of days, as was usual in my experience, from time to time I endured an unpleasant popping and cracking sensation deep inside the ear until finally the discharge of pus ceased and I became, once again, an active member of the three musketeers.

Notwithstanding the last painful episode, with time, the pleasures of those boyhood days at Carshalton seem to merge into a profusion of endless sunny days full of sport and adventure, interrupted by short spells of toil undertaken in order to replenish our pocket-money reserves. Even so, I do recall vividly one very wet occasion during a particularly violent thunderstorm that Billy and I, wearing bathing trunks, unblocked a drain in Aunt Fan's backyard. It was most exciting and we felt so brave, mainly because Aunt Fan and her daughter, Nellie, were so terribly scared. Afterwards, they laughed at our attire, but I felt we were suitably clad for heavy rain.

Despite the expanding built-up areas Carshalton still retained a few patches of its rural past. There were a number of quiet places where sun-dappled waters beckoned us to explore their shallow depths. The ponds were cool to our feet; the streams were positively cold, but we paddled around, ever searching the shadowy world beneath the surface, each with a small net at the end of a long cane: a requisite, which cost only a few coppers.

We netted minnows, stickleback and a rarer member of this dwarfish species, which we kids called a "pottlebelly". Many were the times our attention was attracted to a butterfly — there were far more of them around in those days — and this unfortunate creature, having been caught in the same net we used for fishing, would be received by a budding lepidopterist in exchange for a specimen of the piscine world, which ended up in one of our jam jars. Herein it would live out an all too short life, dying, if not of starvation (boys having lamentably poor memories), by being unceremoniously precipitated down the kitchen sink simply because the jam jar was required for something else, a slug perhaps, or a caterpillar.

In the pursuit of sport there was at our disposal, just across the busy road at the top end of William Street, a large recreation ground where we played both cricket and football on marvellously level and beautifully marked pitches. There were real goal posts, too. And there were no cowpats.

I suppose there were days that were dull and rainy, and these I suspect made up the main bulk of time we spent at cinema shows.

Westerns were favourite. Harold Lloyd and Charlie Chaplin were great, but it was to be a mere girl who induced us to remain seated, first through the early matinée performance, then through a complete second house, before being quietly ejected half way into the third and final performance of the evening.

An amused usherette, acting at the request of a worried Aunt Fan, located and identified us before politely asking us to leave. She explained that we had not broken any rules; it was simply that an elderly lady waiting in the foyer was enquiring as to our whereabouts.

The cinema was in Sutton High Street and Aunt Fan had walked all the way from Carshalton, going out of her way by calling in at another cinema, which was showing an adventure film. She had really not expected us to be looking at the little-girl-cum-great-star, Shirley Temple.

Aunt Fan soon forgave us. We had mentioned we were going to the pictures in Sutton, but we had not stated precisely where. She, for her part, had not expected us to remain in a cinema for over seven hours and had naturally become worried. For our part we begged her not to reveal the fact that we were watching a Shirley Temple film when she found us. Whatever would the boys of William Street think of the three musketeers!

Indeed it was not to Shirley Temple that I lost my young heart. I went for the more mature type. Fay Wray was my darling and I saw "King Kong", the film in which she starred, four times, twice sitting through two performances. I hardly noticed the ape.

I was twelve when I first watched television. This was at a public house in William Street. Every Thursday evening in the largest bar of the Cottage of Content the furniture was arranged so that most of the seating accommodation faced the television set, sited upon a low stage at the far end of the room. Even before the screen lit up it was gazed upon with a reverence more usually accorded to a deeply hallowed shrine and, as the magic moment arrived, the lighting became subdued and all conversation hushed into silence.

I am able to describe what took place within the confines of licensed premises because we, the kids of William Street, were permitted to stand — provided we behaved ourselves — just inside a curtained doorway about half way along the room.

There were always several generous grown-ups in the place and we seldom went long without the offer of a mineral drink, a packet of crisps or perhaps a chocolate wafer or two. I am not at all certain which was the main attraction, the television or the refreshments, but in all it was a good way to wind up the day.

Billy, Georgie and I had many a narrow escape when we went out "scrumping": a popular term for the act of stealing fruit from an orchard or garden. Although we came close to being caught more than once, at no time were we recognised. So, thus far, we had never been sought after by the law with the exception of one memorable incident, but it was not for "scrumping".

Early one lovely Sunday morning, we were about eight at the time, we decided to go for a ramble. Aimlessly we headed towards a place called Hackbridge and from somewhere in its vicinity we sighted on the far horizon what appeared to be a cluster of tiny diamonds scintillating in the morning sun. It was the then gigantic Crystal Palace.

The size of this steel and glass erection may be more easily appreciated if I state that, upon a clear day, reflected sunlight could be seen radiating from this imposing edifice at a point high upon a range of hills just to the north of Midhurst: a distance of more than forty miles. From where we stood we estimated it to be ten miles away. We would ramble aimlessly no more. The Crystal Palace was our goal.

We threaded our way through the streets and back roads of many strange places, often losing sight of our objective. A score of times we retraced our steps until at some vantage point once again we were able to re-orientate ourselves. At last, in the early afternoon, we knew we were getting very close. It was no longer a halo of reflected light; the lines of a colossal building were clearly discernible.

By this time we were, without exception, ravenously hungry. Earlier, we had proposed, once we reached our goal, to travel home by tram or at least the biggest part of the way, for we calculated we had enough money to meet three fares to Croydon and even perhaps a little farther.

Now a crisis had arisen, one that was solved unanimously and promptly. We spent every penny we possessed on chocolate. It was irresistible; we were starving.

Sitting upon a low garden wall, our feet just clear of the pavement, we rested our legs and soon assuaged the hunger pains, not only by means of the chocolate, but with the all-consuming satisfaction of being able to gaze triumphantly at the upper quarters of the Crystal Palace towering above us, even though it was still a good half a mile away.

In the sweltering heat of the afternoon sun we walked on, pausing once to drink deliciously cold water from a wayside fountain and then quite suddenly there it was, just across the road. There in all its icy-looking majesty stood the Crystal Palace.

Its size alone was impressive, yet we were all a little disappointed. I honestly cannot say what I had expected: maybe turrets, battlements, loopholes . . . I know I had the idea that palaces and castles were much the same, but this did not measure up to anything I had in mind.

What I was looking at reminded me of a greenhouse of gigantic proportions. We exchanged proud smiles and with all those twisted miles behind us we had not the heart to express disappointment.

Now the pressing problem was to find a way home. On the outward journey we had had the advantage of a very distinct landmark, even though we had lost sight of it on too many occasions. There was a huge gasholder at Carshalton, quite near William Street in fact, but we could hardly expect to see that from a distance of about ten miles.

One of us noticed that some of the passing trams had Croydon marked upon their destination boards. It was decided to follow the appropriate tramlines in the full knowledge that although it was by no means the shortest route at least we would not be lost.

We plodded on. All joy withered by the afternoon sun and the spirit of adventure abandoned a long way behind us at the site of that steel and glass enticement. It was growing cooler, but since we were growing increasingly weary, the one factor negated the other. By early evening we reached Croydon and we were almost staggering from both hunger and fatigue.

We were spurred on a little as Billy and Georgie began to recognise various buildings along our route. Soon they were familiar with our whereabouts and, leaving the tramlines, we entered the final lap of our marathon journey. Progress was slow for we needed to rest so often, and a nasty blister had developed upon poor Georgie's heel.

When we eventually turned into William Street it was nearly nine o'clock; daylight was fading fast and the street lamps were aglow. Georgie went on up the road to his home; Billy and I went into Aunt Fan's.

Upon entering the little front room there was such a hullabaloo that, had we been fit and able, we would most certainly have run off in fear. There was Aunt Fan, Nellie and Nancy, along with Billy's mother, all talking at once and every word of it directed at us.

We did manage to interject the information that we had just completed a round trip on foot to the Crystal Palace, but this merely incited the surrounding tongues to even more violent action, as expressions of anger, relief and disbelief were wagged out. But we were too weary to care. Even the sudden appearance of a policeman in the open doorway failed to cause us much concern, although he did seem to overcrowd the room a bit.

It transpired that in the early evening Aunt Fan had enlisted the aid of the police by reporting us as missing and they had, of course, been looking out for us. Somehow, despite the fact that most of our homeward journey had been along the main roads they did not spot us, which was a great pity for had we fallen into their hands we would no doubt have received a ride home.

The policeman berated us unmercifully and before he left Aunt Fan, with an unusually straight face, ordered us to bed. Nobody said goodnight to us.

Billy and I almost always shared the little back bedroom at Aunt Fan's during the holidays and when

87

we did, without exception, we went to bed on a supper of apple pie and warm custard. This night we retired exhausted, sad and very hungry.

We crawled into bed and lay there too tired to talk at length, listening vaguely to the exchange of farewells from downstairs until the night grew almost silent. Suddenly — what a joyous, unforgettable moment — Aunt Fan came into the bedroom bearing two steaming dishes. "Best eat this before you fall asleep." We ate ravenously, but I barely remember swallowing the last mouthful.

The sun was high when we awoke the next day, still leg-weary and a little footsore, but otherwise none the worse for our expedition. Georgie proved his mobility by joining us at Aunt Fan's wearing a dressing strapped carefully over his blistered heel. He, too, had been admonished overnight, both by his father and later by the policeman who evidently called upon him after he had left Aunt Fan.

As the day progressed we discovered that we were heroes in the eyes of the neighbourhood. Nancy's husband worked out that we had walked something like twenty-five miles. Quite a feat for eight-year-olds they all agreed.

I told Billy and Georgie that I thought our performance was overrated, bearing in mind that at around the halfway mark we were left with no alternative but to keep walking. Billy told me to shut up, implying that we should bask in glory. So I did.

★ ★ ★

Before concluding my recollections of Carshalton I must refer to the low living standard accepted so philosophically, even cheerfully, by Aunt Fan and, so far as I could see, most of her associates.

Aunt Fan's house was little better than my own, but it did have two proper bedrooms, a backyard of its own and a narrow strip of garden in which stood a private lavatory. Also, despite being in a built-up area, from the front or back door of 60 William Street I was able to see much, much more of the sky than by standing anywhere at Duck Lane, in rural Midhurst.

I was still quite young when I realised there was an enforced financial stratagem operating in William Street: a simple system of borrowing from Peter to pay Paul. The insurance man might reap the benefit of a tallyman's temporary loss, or vice versa, ad infinitum.

When food is cheap, but money scarce, the balance is precarious. I saw Aunt Fan's initiative was sharpened to a fine edge that cut through profit margins to yield a weekly harvest. And I witnessed also she was not alone.

She used to set out, Bill and I often accompanied her, sometimes with the kiddy-cart, at about nine o'clock on a Saturday evening with the chief aim of procuring a bargain by way of a weekend joint. Lack of refrigeration induced the butcher to prefer a few pence on a Saturday night to a possible nothing on a Monday morning when the leftover meat might well be too far gone to sell.

Usually the shop front remained unshuttered until the display slab was empty. It was a brisk, though friendly, business with lots of gaunt-faced women

89

declaring such things as, "I'll take it orf yer 'ands fer a tanner."

"There you are, Fanny dear," the butcher would say, "Ten pence to you and with a pound of sausages thrown in. You'll be the ruin of me."

The greengrocer and the fruiterer, too, had similar problems. Yellowed greens and speckled fruit, which would obviously be unsaleable by Monday, became almost a gift to the late-night shopper. Aunt Fan's pert and winsome manner stood her in good stead and she always collected a heavy load of slightly over-ripe victuals, even if she were on her own.

I have since discovered that she very quickly shared this among the less fortunate members of her community. I do not mean less fortunate in a financial sense, that would be almost impossible, but there were a considerable number of older and less active people living in William Street who were unable to avail themselves of these bargains Aunt Fan provided.

I thoroughly enjoyed the late-night shopping expeditions and it seemed to me that everyone involved did, too, which is proof that poverty does sometimes produce a little light relief. It most certainly produces a great deal of camaraderie.

The reason my holidays at Carshalton were made sumptuous compared to life at home was most of my relatives along with Aunt Fan's close friends were grown-ups, and as a child I was part of a small minority in this fraternity. Consequently there was always the danger of them spoiling me with so many little treats and excursions. But children of my class did not expect to receive something for nothing, at least not very often, and we accepted without question the need to work for pocket money.

The first holiday at Carshalton was drawing to a close and I was feeling sad. It would be nice to see my family and my hometown pals, but after a whole month I had grown quite fond of my holiday surroundings and associates. Only one thing cheered me. The prospect of the journey.

With the aid of guards and porters I found my way home. Mother and my sister, Daisy, met me at the station and at once I was happy again. Keen to know if my young brother could yet manage the blue pedal-car: eager to see my new baby sister and wondering if Father's hand was as good as new.

I soon settled in the old surroundings and into a familiar way of life, which included a return to school, for the autumn term had just begun.

CHAPTER
EIGHT

From 1928–1938:
Farmed Out

At school, the structure regarding the teachers and their respective classes remained the same throughout my entire school life. Apart, that is, from a slight reshuffle brought about by the retirement of my first teacher, Miss Bennett, and the appointment of a new teacher.

Miss Attree was put in charge of the infant class. Miss Parker dealt with the advanced infants, as well as the first real academic class, Standard One. Miss Whittington took Standards Two and Three, and the newly appointed Miss McClellan presided over Standards Four and Five. Mr. Purser, the headmaster, excelled them all: in his room he taught the remaining three Standards: Six, Seven and X-Seven.

At the very least each room seated thirty pupils, and the staff were certainly not pampered by the conditions under which they taught. That each of those teachers managed to maintain such firm discipline whilst effectively instructing two classes at one time, in Mr. Purser's case three, amazes me to this day. Indeed, at least once a week a small contingent of Mr. Purser's boys practised woodwork at the far end of Miss McClellan's room. It was the only place in the school building with space enough to permit the installation of two workbenches. This must have created a bit of a problem for poor Miss McClellan. Imagine explaining a decimal sum to the accompaniment of a non-musical saw.

There were no staff room, no canteen, and the lavatories were across the yard at the rear of the school, with no washing facilities. Although there were the two cloakrooms at the front of the school with a wash basin in each, both surmounted with a wall mirror circumscribed with the maxim: "Cleanliness is next to Godliness". It was really misleading, or was I alone in thinking that to reach Heaven, all one needed to do was wash frequently.

At the age of seven I was in Miss Parker's room and doing quite well in Standard One. It was in this class that I was to learn, among many things, the meaning of the expression "labour in vain", albeit in my case, mental labour.

It was nearing Christmas and every year at this time the children, selected by their teachers to represent the individual classes, would be rehearsing for the annual variety show. The first night, which was also the last, was presented upon the stage in front of the cinema screen at the public hall in North Street.

I was given the leading role in Miss Parker's contribution. I completely forget the essence of the

sketch, but I well remember learning most painstak-
ingly, about twenty four-line verses of poetry. After
several weeks of hard work I was word and gesture
perfect.

That my parents were proud of me needs little
comment. They listened and watched, and sometimes
advised, as I rehearsed hour after hour at home and
they were certain that their young star would shine just
as brightly on the night.

Alas, only a week before the great day, the whole
project was suddenly cancelled. I do not recall the
reason, but the disappointment was nigh unbearable. I
do know that the public hall remained functional and
that the stage had not collapsed, for my mother took
me to see a comedy film on the very evening in the very
place that I was to have made my stage debut.

It was Mother's way of softening one of fate's early
blows, and it was highly successful for, despite the
venue, I soon forgot everything, at least temporarily, as
I entered into the spirit of the film. The school never
again booked the public hall, and I never again dabbled
in the Thespian arts.

Soon after Christmas my ears were very troublesome. A
cold would almost certainly spark off an ear infection
and, since colds are more prevalent in the winter, it was
to me the season of earache. Before spring I underwent
another surgical operation. A further portion of tonsil
and adenoid was carved off, but, as in the earlier
experience, the success was short-lived.

Again the use of chloroform was my principal fear and again it was employed despite my heroic struggle, and a valiant attempt to hold my breath at the same time. When I regained consciousness there was the usual short period of sickness, followed naturally with a sore throat that healed rapidly under repeated applications of ice-cream, jelly and blancmange. Except for the chloroform, it was well worthwhile having the operation.

During this period of my young life I used to stay for quite long spells with two great favourites, Aunt Daisy and her husband, Uncle Ern. Aunt Daisy was my mother's sister and I suppose I was farmed out in order to give Mother a break. With one or the other of us being sick or recuperating from an operation, life was for her a bit of a trial. In fact it was about this time that my sister, Daisy, underwent with complete success an operation for mastoiditis.

Aunt Daisy and Uncle Ern lived in rooms at the highest point of Church Hill, a short walk from Duck Lane along a semi-circular route. But it was even less far if one climbed the tall and crumbling wall to the side of the drying ground near Nan's place: a precarious walk along the top of a couple of garden walls brought one to a point from which it was possible to drop down into Aunt Daisy's backyard.

Many a time I used this short cut instead of walking round by the conventional course, and many were the times I was yelled at by irate tenants and owners as I passed by their properties: not for the fact that I was

95

trespassing, but in my own interests, for the wall route was very dangerous. A fall from a number of places would have resulted in at least a broken body, if not worse. I saved only a minute or two by using this route, so that it had to be the excitement alone that attracted me.

Uncle Ern (I am certain I never once heard him called Ernest) was a lorry driver. He drove for the local mill, at that time grinding with water-powered machinery, and most of his work involved fairly long journeys. There were occasions when he would leave very early in the morning and not return until late the following day.

During the shorter breaks from school — the long summer holiday was always reserved for Carshalton — I would often accompany Uncle Ern on his day trips mostly to the dockyard area of London.

His big Dennis lorry was loaded overnight with a mountain of heavily laden sacks of flour, all stacked under the huge canopy that covered virtually the whole of the vehicle. The lorry waited for morning, in a garage at the end of a narrow yard flanked on both sides with channels of swift-flowing water.

Very early in the morning, sometimes it was still dark, we would stride down North Street towards the mill. It was not far and I was soon sitting excitedly next to Uncle Ern in the driving cab. At that hour of the day it seemed to me that the mill was still sleeping off the effects of yesterday's toil. All was strangely quiet, except for the familiar sound of the nearby waterfall.

The moment Uncle Ern started the engine everything else sprang to life. Moorhens along the river squawked with fright, ducks quacked agitatedly and, in the aureole of light set up by the headlamps, could be seen scores of birds, big and small, shooting skywards in alarm, temporarily forsaking their warm nests.

We usually covered the initial few miles in the first light of dawn, headlamps pointing our way, and then, quite suddenly, the twin beams were no longer required. The sun was illuminating the world: revealing new contours, near and far, at every bend in the road.

It was still early morning when we entered London and we reached Rotherhithe Tunnel before there was any great press of traffic. This was the reason for having started out so early, although there was always a strong company of heavy vehicles converging at this point and at this hour.

I was a little scared of the tunnel for I knew it ran under the Thames, and early in the morning it always seemed to be gleaming wet. Uncle Ern assured me that it was only wet because it was purposely flushed clean by water, but I was never convinced and as we passed through my eyes were constantly on the alert for the least sign of a leak.

In the course of these excursions I saw a lot of the dockland area of London. We would unload at one dockside and then moving on to another we collected a return load, which was usually cattle food called cow-cake and I remember that it contained a lot of linseed oil. It reminded me, in appearance, of countless battered OXO cubes, and I often nibbled away at a

97

piece as we drove along. It did me no apparent harm, although it certainly possessed no ambrosial qualities. I speak only for myself, not for the animals for whom it was intended.

We spent far more time waiting for attention at the dockside than we ever spent in motoring, and it was whilst enduring such a state of immobility that I saw more sparrows gathered in one place than I had ever seen before. The road, the lorries, which formed a long queue, and even the surrounding air was taken over by noisy, greedy sparrows in their thousands. Here was I, a country boy, and I had witnessed nothing like it.

I suppose there was in the backs of most of the lorries a residue of chaff of one kind or another. On the ground there were also spillings of corn and the like. These sparrows were very partial to bread and cheese and were spoilt by the lorry drivers as they opened their lunch packs, whilst waiting in the queue.

These feathered city dwellers would hop through an open window and bounce around the cab without a trace of fear, taking food quite confidently from an outstretched hand. One could almost make playmates of them, and I sadly reflected that country birds were so much more timid.

It was during one of these long waits that I witnessed an odd and well-remembered incident. The day was hot and the cab had become uncomfortably warm, although Uncle Ern seemed happy enough, head lolling against the side window, enjoying an after-sandwiches nap despite the noisy sparrows all around. So as not to disturb him I opened the door very quietly and slid to the ground, latching instead of slamming it behind me. The cool breeze coming off the river was most refreshing and I strolled across to a low wall overlooking the water.

I leaned over and was surprised to find that there was a considerable drop on the other side, perhaps fifteen feet or so. Directly beneath me, about four feet out from the wall lay a large, flat-topped barge moored fore and aft to a couple of big iron rings set in the lower part of the embankment. The water was very shallow along the base of the wall, and barely covered a bed of filthy-looking mud. The sound of strange and strident voices came from a small cabin at the rear of the vessel.

To the right and left of me there was nothing of any great interest, just the wall ranging along the river and disappearing eventually on both sides in a maze of dockside berths and buildings. Except for the conglomerate but distant drone of various industrial activities and the almost silent passage of an occasional vessel way out in the mid stream of the river, all in my near vicinity was still and peaceful. Even the alien voices had died away.

There was a sudden squeal, the barge below me exploded into a scene of violent action. A man was staggering backwards from the open doorway of the cabin. A split second later a billhook came into view, held menacingly shoulder high by another man whom I recognised instantly to be Chinese. I had seen quite a few Chinamen in and around Limehouse, but not one as ugly as this.

The first figure had turned around and I saw that he, too, was Chinese. He scuttled down the length of the deck, and reaching the bow could do no more than swing round and face his assailant who was in very close pursuit. He threw up his arms in apparent supplication, but the armed man came on. They were in close contact, but I am certain the billhook was not used, when the frightened man fell backwards over the side, down into the oozing mire between the barge and the wall beneath me. He made a mighty splash as he struck the surface flat on. In moments he was standing upright, waist deep, in black mud and filthy water. Although he did not appear to be hurt, he was unmistakeably yelling for help.

The Chinaman on deck seemed to undergo a complete change of heart. Dropping the billhook he rushed off and from somewhere near the cabin fetched a rickety ladder, which he carefully lowered over the side, inviting his compatriot to come aboard. I did not witness the outcome, for as the ugly Chinaman slid the ladder into the water he caught sight of me.

I was going through that part of life when to me all Chinamen looked sinister, but never before had I gazed upon such an evil countenance. For a few seconds I was mesmerized by this close up look at him: a pair of eyes, half closed yet glinting ominously, a crooked nose that I bet had been broken more than once, and a thin snakelike mouth framed by a long and narrow, traditionally oriental, moustache. I broke the spell and ran as though for my life to the safety of the lorry.

It is no exaggeration when I say that for many years to come my adjudication of whatever went on in China was governed by the memory of both that evil face and the deadly looking billhook.

At that age I was quite able to read the newspapers and, although I did not know a Nationalist from a Communist with regard to their political aims, I was aware that a civil war in China would reduce her population. Japan, too, was busily engaged in this undertaking. I imagined thousands of slaughtered Chinamen lying in heaps with their rusting billhooks scattered all around.

A couple of months before my eighth birthday Aunt Daisy produced a little Ernie, but it was earlier in that same year that, as a boy, I was to see for the last time how the other half lived.

Not more than fifty yards from Aunt Daisy's place there lived a retired colonel, who entertained friends fairly frequently at his large and comfortable home. If there were a dinner-party, Aunt Daisy would sometimes help wait at table and would also assist with all general domestic duties.

She was very friendly with the colonel's housekeeper and whenever he was away on holiday or business Aunt Daisy and I would move into the house to provide company for her, especially at night. This arrangement worked most conveniently, for Uncle Ern was often away on an overnight journey.

The luxury of ice-cold milk, handed to me from the interior of the first refrigerator I ever saw, remains a

101

blissful memory. And, what is more, I was allowed a whole pint at a time if I so desired! There was lemonade, too, also ice-cold and with an exquisite flavour.

There was always plenty of fresh fruit: a variety of it, and permission to eat it readily given, even peaches and cream for elevenses. Then there was the fudge, the most delicious sweetmeat in the world, or so I thought, made for me by the housekeeper herself.

Breakfast seemed a grand affair: fruit juice, cereal, followed by a cooked meal. I tried a kidney one morning, but after one bite I concluded that I much preferred a sausage. There was a choice of tea or coffee, or I could always quaff more of that seemingly inexhaustible supply of milk.

In fact all meals were a grand affair, even though we took them in the kitchen. And at the end of the day, after an enjoyable bath — and I mean it — in a great slippery tub containing such a volume of water one could almost float in it, I went contentedly off to bed with a book and a steaming mug of Ovaltine. There were a number of times that I found myself comparing that bath with the humble tin bath, which, when not in use, hung indecorously outside upon the rear wall of the scullery at Duck Lane.

In this lovely house, the room designated as a library fascinated me. It was a large room with many shelves holding many books lining the walls almost to the ceiling. This was the place, which might well have been the original influence in my subsequent lack of interest in comic-papers. There were lots of books far above my comprehension, but there were a few novels by Edgar Wallace, and before I was eight I had already read "The Four Just Men" and at least a couple more of that prolific writer's books.

There was another room, richly furnished, in which I would stand gazing, almost in awe, at a variety of glistening, elegantly shaped decanters containing mostly amber-coloured liquids. Along with these stood several elaborately-labelled bottles and all kinds of beautifully designed glasses, cut so finely that miniature stars seemed to twinkle in all directions. (Another original influence?)

I could not but help think of those very ordinary looking bottles that adorned the landing at the foot of the bed in Duck Lane and which bore neat little labels in my mother's handwriting proclaiming the contents to be "Cowslip 31" or "Parsnip 30", and so on. I thought, too, of the bottle of cheap port wine that I had seen at Christmas times upon the table in our front room and which mother referred to as: "My little treat". Of course, I was unaware at the time it was a cheap wine, but knowing our normal financial position I might well have guessed it. Our glasses, too, just did not compare with the glasses that so often riveted my attention in that infinitely more luxurious abode.

Every time I stayed there I knew I was being spoilt and I revelled in it. I loved to just wander around this spacious house, feeling the thick carpeting with feet more accustomed to the solidity of a linoleum covered brick floor. At home we did not possess upholstered furniture: here I was able to select an armchair which I would sink into before marvelling at its comfortable, shifting contours.

Often, after sitting awhile in one of these snug chairs I worried about the effects it might have upon my young back. Father, you see, whenever she complained that her Windsor chair was uncomfortable, frequently told my mother that the stupidly designed modern armchairs were obviously bad for the spine, and that we should consider ourselves fortunate in possessing hard straight-backed chairs. I am sure Mother did not find this consolation at all gratifying, for all she ever said in reply was "Oh, yes!".

Anyway, after several visits to this sumptuous house and finding my back as good as ever, I took every advantage of my surroundings. There was nothing I liked more, especially on a wet day, than to disappear in one of those commodious armchairs, in one hand a lump of fudge, and in the other a good book. The real world and all its tedium exchanged for the fears and thrills to be found between the covers of an adult novel.

Young as I was, I decided there and then, this was the life for me. I wished not that the colonel had been my father, but that my father had been the colonel.

To me these quarters were beyond compare, but I also appreciated that Aunt Daisy's home was considerably more comfortable than mine at Duck Lane. It was furnished just that little better, too, for Uncle Ern had been in full employment since leaving the army. Lorry driving was a good job in those days, possibly because there were not that many drivers about.

I was always happy to stay at Aunt Daisy's place. The lavatory was outside, but it was private. There was no bathroom, but then there seldom was in a working-class home, and we — like the majority — found the old tin bath sufficed. Gaslight I found was nicer to read by than the oil lamps and candles I had been used to at Duck Lane.

Outside there was a cement-paved drying ground, a little garden and just by the back door a small yard where I spent hours at a time kicking a ball against a wall, much to the perplexity of a chemist whose shop was on the inner side of the wall. However, once he discovered the source and reason for the almost incessant thumping noise he merely said, "Play on, son".

We occupied the entire rear of the house and upstairs, overlooking both yard and garden were our two fair-sized bedrooms. I shared the matrimonial room, sleeping in a small bed lined against the far wall.

The other bedroom was rented to a lodger, a man by the name of Bill. He was a dustman by profession and he also took care of the gigantic grey horse, which pulled the cart.

There was one slight drawback to this arrangement (but it did not cross my mind at that time); in order to gain access to his room Bill had to pass right through the matrimonial bedroom. Years passed before I realised what a discreet gentleman he must have been.

Even after the birth of young Ernie I was still treated in the same way by both aunt and uncle; that is in the manner of an only child, with all the attendant benefits and little luxuries.

For example, it was Uncle Ern's habit to go out for a drink before Sunday dinner, just as Uncle Harry and I used to, and he always returned with a big bag of chocolate buttons to be shared later between Aunty Daisy and me whilst he enjoyed his forty — or was it forty dozen? — winks. It seems to me now that Aunt Daisy and I did little more on a Sunday afternoon than to sit and read, munching delicious chocolate buttons. Home in Duck Lane a similar amount of sweets would not have lasted a quarter of the time.

Aunt Daisy possessed a small bookcase and it contained lots of maroon coloured hardback books; they were rather small, too, but were quite easily readable. I believe this series of novels was then obtainable at Woolworth's. By the age of thirteen I had read almost every book that Edgar Wallace had written. I was also well versed in the intricacies of the Turf, having read a number of novels about horseracing by, I think, Nat Gould.

A memory, which still brings a smile from long ago, was born of a baby-sitting occasion on a dark winter's evening.

Just across the room Ernie was sound asleep in his pram. My aunt and uncle would be back in just over the hour, and I was deeply engrossed in a thrilling novel entitled "The Wrecker".

I was about ten at the time, every now and again I felt the hairs upon my neck stand stiffly to attention as yet another passage in the book scared the wits out of me. It was certainly a chilling tale, but curiosity repeatedly overcame fear and I refused to respond to the instinct that told me to put the book down.

The house at Church Hill was not really spooky at all, but I could always scare myself a little if I wanted. An ottoman, a rather large one, stood just outside an inner door of the front room, in a passage that led to the stairway. I regarded this piece of furniture uneasily, but almost every time I passed it I just had to lift the padded lid and peep in. After all, my reading indicated that a trunk was a most likely place in which to find a dead body.

The ottoman belonged to an elderly lady who occupied a room at the front of the building, and all I ever came across were a few folded blankets and miscellaneous items of clothing. Peeping into it always produced mixed feelings of disappointment and relief.

It was always very quiet at the back of the house. The only sound so far this evening was the comforting, incessant hissing, emanating from the gaslight. A muffled tearing sound came from behind the inner door; I dropped the book in alarm. Dead quiet for a moment and, then again, the same sound. Having been engrossed in a book such as "The Wrecker" at the time my nerves were already frayed. Calling up what little courage remained, I moved towards the door. I had no reason to listen intently, the same muffled noise grew no louder, but it seemed to intensify as though something or someone had reached a point of frenzy. My hand rested clammily upon the doorknob. My

107

throat was dry and my forehead damp; then came, once again, silence.

This was as disconcerting as the noise. I just had to know what was happening out there in the corridor. I threw open the door; light from behind me streamed into the unlit passage, but there was nothing unusual to be seen. And then, from within the ottoman, it came again: the same tearing sound, but even more frantic.

Not quite petrified, and using up the very last dregs of a fast leaking heroism, I slowly raised the lid of the trunk. I could see little for I was standing directly in the path of light. This compelled me to lift the lid higher and, as I was in the process of moving to one side, there was a sudden movement from within. Something leapt towards me, landed on my shoulder quite lightly and was away into the front room like a bat out of hell.

I spun round and there upon the hearth-rug looking as terrified as me stood the big black cat that belonged to the elderly lady whose trunk it was. I opened the back door and the cat rushed into the darkness without so much of a mew of thanks. I was unaware until I later undressed for bed that I had received a couple of not too serious scratches along my shoulder.

At the moment I felt nothing of this. The nerve-racking ordeal had left me very shaken. But worse, I suspected that somehow fear had affected my sight for I was certain the gaslight was on the wane. Aunt Daisy always made sure that there were plenty of pennies in the meter. It was usually the last thing she attended to before going out and I was fully aware of this. On the other hand if she had overlooked this small

108

but important duty, and if the light went out, I had not a single penny to my name.

After a little while my panic subsided enough for me to think that perhaps my imagination was playing tricks for, apart from an occasional slight flicker, the light burned on. But I was still nervous and I most certainly did not relish the thought of baby-sitting in the dark. Before I settled down again, a very optimistic aspiration at the time, there were things to be done.

Aunt Daisy and Uncle Ern arrived home, right on schedule, to find me still reading "The Wrecker", but with a lighted candle on either side of me, despite the gaslight, which had continued burning brightly throughout.

CHAPTER
NINE

The Ice Hole

For reasons best known to grown-ups, these happy sojourns would come to an end and I was returned to Duck Lane and grim reality. Back to the beetles, the militant fleas, the dusty Keating's Powder and the smelly oil lamps and candles — to say nothing of the communal lavatories.

I adapted to it all quickly, and I was soon exercising old skills, such as crushing black beetles with a club-hammer. We got into a filthy state, for the venue of this particular sport was in the coal cupboard under the stairs: a dark place, until floodlit by candlelight. The butchery took place mostly when the weather was inclement and Mother was temporarily absent, out shopping for instance. I was always severely reprimanded upon her return, even more so when I invited my brother to try his young hand at this vicious sport. Coated with coal dust we looked like a couple of chimney sweeps, yet I always kidded myself, when daring to do it again, that this time I would keep clean. This was impossible, and finally Mother told Father; that ended it.

★ ★ ★

I was eight years old. Little Cecil had taken over the blue pedal-car altogether, it being far too small for me. Father continued my boxing lessons, but not so entertainingly as the sessions with Uncle Harry. Uncle Mossy still took me on long rambles from time to time. And my eldest sister, Daisy, was of great assistance to Mother at that time, especially when it came to taking care of our baby sister, Marjorie, who had reached the age of one without illness.

This was a favourable but short part of our childhood when it seemed for once we were all together; that is to say, nobody was being ill or operated upon at the time.

I had a narrow escape from serious injury when attempting to knock a nail into a piece of wood. Foolishly, I used the top of the fireguard for a workbench. I accidentally struck the handle of a saucepan, standing upon the hob, with a heavy blow from my over-large hammer. The saucepan upturned violently in my direction. Luckily, most of the potatoes and boiling water missed me, but my legs were soon covered with a mass of blisters caused by the splash. Very painful!

Another frightening incident also concerning water occurred at about this time. It happened during a short visit to the uncle and aunt who lived in the wood near Petworth. I was in their garden leaning over a nearly full water-butt watching lots of strange, tiny creatures swimming around just below the surface of the murky and rather nasty smelling water, when my sister, Daisy, in simple fun, upended me. I plunged head first into the barrel. There was just not room enough for me to alter my position, so I remained, head down, legs threshing the air.

This humble autobiography could not be written had my mother not been nearby. She responded promptly to my frightened sister's cries, and I was hauled from the water-butt by my feet. I think I was truly half drowned for as much water poured from inside me as drained from my saturated clothing, and Mother continued to hold me upside-down for a few moments for this very reason.

Daisy, quite bravely, owned up to pushing me, but, as I recall, she was not too severely punished. The realisation of what had almost happened, in the pursuit of fun, was in itself enough to dissuade an encore. In spite of the filthy water I suffered no ill effects, but I never again leaned over a barrel without first looking behind me.

My eighth birthday was spent at Carshalton and I was again attending school in Midhurst after a splendid summer holiday. Autumn was fast approaching when several schools in the district, including mine, were closed down for at least a week due to a widespread epidemic of scarlet fever.

I, for one, did not rejoice, for I was fond of school and it seemed rather pointless since we invariably sought each other out and played around together in small gangs.

Once when strolling along West Street on my own I met up with a schoolboy of about my age. His name was Bill and he lived near the Wheatsheaf, a place I had never visited since the death of poor Uncle Harry. Acknowledging we were both at a loose end we decided to go for a ramble, heading for no real reason in the direction of St Anne's Hill. We sat for a short time on the low wall overlooking the river, idly yarning and watching the steady progress of two swans far below us as they swam against the current.

I do not recall whose suggestion it was, but we decided to explore the icehouse: a cave-cum-well in the side of a neighbouring hill. It was assumed that this cold storage area had been part of the facilities of the nearby ill-fated mansion, "Cowdray Ruins".

Guarding the entrance to the cave was a three-barred fence, obviously erected to prevent cattle wandering in, for all the adjacent meadows were pastureland, with the exception of a couple of polo grounds.

It was a cloudy day, which did not help. We climbed over the fence and peered into the gloomy interior. The ceiling, not far above our heads, was of arched brickwork, and ran six or seven yards into the side of the hill. The floor disappeared abruptly not very far from the entrance in what can only be described as a shallow well.

Bill possessed three safety matches in a very worn box. He struck one and we gazed to the extreme edge of its radiance, barely making out the bottom of the shaft. It all looked more than a little unsafe. Over the years a lot of bricks and brickbats had fallen from the ceiling and the sides, and at that time constituted an extremely rough floor some ten feet below us.

Lying on his stomach with his head hanging well over the edge Bill struck a second match, this time holding it down at arm's length. "Crumbs, there's summat there," and then excitedly he cried, "Come here! Look! It's a body of some sort! I can see its eyes!"

I was kneeling at Bill's side. I did not see the body, only two points of reflected light that might well have come from a pair of eyes. Bill dropped the near burnt out match; unfortunately the flame died before it reached the bottom, leaving us in a shadowy half-light. We moved to the entrance and, sitting on the fence, we held a conference.

This was the first time either of us had dared to enter the icehouse. It was off the beaten track, and, as younger children, we had regarded the cave in the hillside from afar with a chilling concern. We had loved being frightened by stories of ogres and witches and the like, who surely would dwell in such a place. Our elders had scared us with eerie tales about all sorts of hillside tenants, as we in turn would scare our juniors.

Bill and I were old enough to debunk all the fantasy attached to our dark surroundings. There was danger here: it lay in the crumbling bricks and mortar, which threatened imminent, total collapse of both tunnel and well and the risk of stumbling or slipping into its depths. A decision had to be made: whether or not to walk away and forever wonder about the body in the shaft.

One live match remained. We could easily climb down and take a close look. Bill quite wisely suggested that it would be prudent if one of us were to remain in the tunnel, just in case we found it impossible to climb back up. I agreed.

We tossed a halfpenny. It fell to my lot to climb down. With the one remaining match safely in its box in my jacket pocket I went over the edge.

Despite the darkness it was not very difficult and there were plenty of handholds, although a lot of them came away from the wall to fall with a thud beneath me. I just hoped nothing fell from the roof. I reached the bottom quite easily and staggered about on what was, literally, a pile of bricks. I groped around for the body before I struck the match. "It's furry and cold," I reported, "And I think it's a dog."

The light of the match proved me right. There lay the corpse of a fully-grown black spaniel, wearing a brown leather collar. Before the match was spent, I moved the dog just a little. There was a faintly malodorous smell, but putrefaction had not yet set in to any great extent. "I suppose we ought to get it up. Somebody might be lookin' for it."

"Yea, we'll 'ave to get a rope or some string. I expect we could pull it up."

"We'll need more matches, too, it's pretty black down 'ere."

Eagerly, I attempted to climb out. I could only just discern the brick face, and was quite unable to determine where the safe handholds might be. Coming down I had had gravity on my side; on the ascent it was most decidedly against me. The more I clawed upwards, the more bricks I dislodged. I was in trouble and near to panic. "I can't make it, Bill." My voice was

115

tremulous and not much above a whisper, for I had read of avalanches precipitated by the mere cry of a human voice. I was scared of only one thing, that the whole place might cave in. I said as much to Bill.

I could tell by the strained tone of his voice that he, too, was worried, if not so frightened as I. "I'll 'ave to get a rope and some more matches. I'll be as quick as I can."

We were not far from home, so provided that the necessary articles were soon gathered, I would not have more than an eternity to wait. How I prayed for Bill's safe return, coupled with the fervent hope that he did not forget what he was about. I tried just once more to climb up, but a small fall of bricks petrified me. I stood in the dark bowels of the earth quaking in my shoes and scarcely daring to breathe, waiting to be crushed to death, to lie forever beside the body of an unknown dog. I felt sick with terror. There was nothing I could do but wait.

When I heard Bill's voice I almost collapsed with relief, and his shadow darkening the semi-circle of light above me was the most welcome sight of my young life. He had managed to obtain some more matches (in fact he had pinched his mother's from off the gas stove) and a long length of hairy looking string. It was strong, and doubled served as a rope. He lowered my lifeline, tying the other end to the fence.

By then I had lost all interest in the dog. My one ambition was to get up and out of this ghastly hole.

"Tie your end of the string to the dog's collar," said Bill, lighting a match at the same time, and completely disregarding the state of my nerves.

"What the 'ell . . ." I started to object, but then, in spite of my fears, it did not seem a bad idea. It would only take a second or two, and it would make it all worthwhile.

I looped the string through the collar and made fast. Fast, too, was I in making my exit from this tomb of gloom. Climbing was still awkward, but by clutching the string the bricks falling from beneath my feet were of no great worry. Bill helped me over the edge and I immediately made my way towards light and blessed fresh air. The poor animal didn't give off much smell. The whole interior had a dank and musty odour that, in the excitement of it all, I had not really noticed until the moment of my rescue.

I leaned for a long time against the top rail of the fence, my legs refused to stop trembling. I wanted to run away from this awful place at top speed.

Bill, meanwhile, was trying to pull up the dog on his own. "It's too darned heavy." Reluctantly, I turned and left my sanctuary at the entrance, and moving into the shadows again, I rejoined Bill.

It was not so dangerous at this level; if anything untoward happened, we could always run for it. I had heard the derogatory term dog's body used by many a grown-up, then I felt fully justified in using it in the same manner against this unfortunate creature whose corpse we were about to raise from its grave. It had very nearly caused me to suffer a complete nervous

117

breakdown. I felt it was still touch and go with me. There was only one aim, one consolation, for only the completion of the plan would serve as recompense for my sufferings.

We began to haul on the string.

It was not easy, the carcass was much heavier than anticipated, and to make things worse it kept snagging up under projections of broken brickwork. At last the head came within reach and we were soon able to grasp the thick, black coat. I was glad, for it looked too much as though we were hanging the poor animal, as it came into view suspended by the neck at the end of our string.

We both had a firm grip on it, and puffing and panting we rolled the body up and over the edge. "Phew, it smells a bit," gasped Bill.

This was indisputably true. As we picked up the poor creature by its legs and carried it towards the entrance, we could see no clear signs of decomposition. This led us to conjecture how long the animal had been at the bottom of the shaft. Had it fallen accidentally or had a particularly callous, so-called human being deliberately pushed it to its ultimate death? We doubted that the fall would kill a dog instantly, so starvation was the probable cause of death.

All the ifs and buts were discussed. Supposing we had come along a day or so earlier. Would we have discovered a terrified spaniel in the process of enduring a lonely, ghastly end? How we wished we might have brought it up alive.

Of course, it might have died a natural death and been thrown down the shaft by an owner who could not be bothered to dig a grave. We doubted this, for to have carried such a weight from even the nearest house would have demanded more exertion than was required to dig a suitable hole.

No, we finally decided that the luckless dog had sniffed its way in from the meadow and had fallen, jumped or scrambled its way down the wall of the shaft. Yes, we agreed, it might have descended out of doggy curiosity; never realising there was no way of return. I particularly shuddered at the thought.

We were very nearly in tears before we decided to place the body just outside the fence, where a searching owner might see it. We would also spread the word around, so that he or she might hear of it. We discussed all probabilities before leaving and then, feeling very sad for the dog, but very pleased with ourselves, wandered homewards.

Our route took us across the market square, on the far side of which stood a public house called the Swan. As we approached, a man came slowly down the flight of stone steps, which protruded from the near side of the building. I knew from experience that men in pubs did lots of talking, so urging Bill to lengthen his stride, I hurried up to the man. I looked up at him, noting that he had a twinkle in his smallish eyes and, I suspected, a lot of beer in his biggish belly. I told him about our exploit and asked if he knew of anyone who had lost a dog, at the same time giving him a detailed description of the animal. He shook his head. No, but he would keep his ears open. Bill and I went home.

A couple of days later, when a gang of us was busily enacting the battle of Spion Kop on the summit of St Anne's Hill, an elderly, shabbily-dressed man came over and asked if I were one of the boys who had discovered the dead dog. He said I fitted the description given by a man at the Swan.

I nodded and called out to Bill, who was playing the part of a Boer at the time, to come on over.

The man's face was a mass of wrinkles and he looked very sad. "Well nippers, I 'oped I'd find yer to say thanks. I s'pose the poor feller wandered into the place and fell down the soddin' well. What an end for my old mate. The bloody 'ole should be filled in — excuse my language. 'E went missin' over a week ago, an' I bin lookin' fer 'im ever since. 'E be buried in my garden now. I fetched 'im 'ome yest'y mornin'."

At this point I think we all felt like crying. In fact I am certain I saw tears begin to glisten in the old man's eyes. He turned away and over his shoulder he declared, "One of these days, when me ship comes 'ome, I'll reward yer both fer what yer done. At least yer put me mind at rest."

But there was little doubt, as time passed, that his ship had foundered.

CHAPTER
TEN

Bright Hour

The scarlet fever epidemic was over and we were back at school, but for me, alas, not for long. My ears, especially my left one, were giving me severe attacks of pain and seemingly endless trouble and I missed a lot of schooling during the term. Christmas was almost upon us before there came a respite from my torment, and all who took an interest in my academic progress were pleasantly surprised when I gained third place in the end of term examination.

Before the end of the holidays the accursed ear trouble flared up again and plagued me, almost continuously, until winter surrendered to spring. There were times, and this is absolutely true, that the agony and misery caused by those internal abscesses drove me, not yet nine years old, to my knees where I prayed that I might soon die.

Many were the times a doctor was sent for, but he could do little more than watch out for signs of possible malignant complications, such as mastoiditis. The salt-bag, needless to say, was always near to hand, and nothing the doctor could produce was an improvement upon that. During the spring the number of attacks decreased, and I often went as long as a month without a major earache occurring. Except for the acknowledgement that one caught fewer colds than in winter, it remains a mystery why.

Between the bouts of ear trouble it was not all school and play. A visit to the local cinema necessitated earning the entrance fee. This was achieved in much the same way as when at Carshalton, although it involved a much harder and dirtier enterprise. Father possessed a small wooden truck; no more than a strong, oblong box set upon a pair of iron wheels, it was a very useful vehicle. There were two shafts at one end to pull it along, rather as a horse pulls a cart. Its main function was to carry home the allotment produce from June Lane, especially the potato harvest; and in the winter it was used to carry the logs from the weather-beaten saw-horse that stood at the far end of the drying ground, as though rooted to the spot. When not in use the truck was parked close by, protected from the elements by a piece of old linoleum.

With the help of a mate (young Dick often assisted me and in later years Cecil when his health permitted) I was able to transport sacks of coke from the gasworks, for a small consideration, to the homes of those who requested it. The gasworks was not far away; it lay just below the southern slopes of St Anne's Hill, beautifully tucked away on what had once been a busy wharf side. Nearby there ran a narrow, gurgling brook where once had been a wide stretch of water, and here and there the rotting remains of canal barges rose untidily from the muddy surrounds. But there were no problems for wheeled mobility, for the road to the gasworks was wide and well made.

This coke delivery enterprise was carried out on Saturday mornings. First, of course, I brought home our own requirements for a week, and then, looking very professional with the truck drawn up alongside, I would hammer upon local doors canvassing for customers who needed to do nothing more than produce an average size sack and ready money.

The sack was always well filled, with just enough slack left to tie it securely with string. The charge made for the coke was sixpence (2½p) and our minimum fee for freighting it was one penny, but I must say we very often received twopence.

Sometimes, when the men were busy inside the main building at the gasworks, we would have to wait for attention, but this was never boring. We used to stand just inside a huge doorway and watch the men, armed with long rods, draw out the red-hot coke from the furnaces. Water was then thrown over it, and through the clouds of steam we could just discern the fires darkening a little as they were re-stoked with heaps of coal.

Our sacks were not filled here, for the coke first had to be carted in an iron wheelbarrow to a huge pile that lay on the far side of the wide front yard, where it cooled down altogether. From the coolest perimeter of this heap a man using a many pronged fork filled our sacks and took the money.

My ear trouble often created a secondary nuisance. Having built up a thriving transport business, I would go down with an ear infection, leaving the door of opportunity wide open to others. Some of my customers remained faithful, like Nan, Aunt Daisy and, naturally, my mother, so I always found a small foundation of clients on which to rebuild my business.

There was one cinema programme daily. It started promptly at seven-fifteen and ended at about ten o'clock. There were two different programmes each week, Monday to Wednesday and Thursday to Saturday, and unless there was a particularly good film on during the first half of the week, Friday and Saturday were the most popular evenings for the younger children. It meant a late night was not followed by the need to get up reasonably early for school.

It was customary for most children to attend church on a Sunday morning. This did not necessitate rising at an early hour. My family provided no exceptions to this rule and as we each grew old enough we went to both morning and afternoon service. Frankly, I am not too certain as to the reason for our good attendance record, but I rather feel it was more to get us out from under our parents' feet than a motivation based upon purely religious aims.

Although the Rev. Tatchell continued to spend a lot of time abroad, I saw him in the pulpit on many occasions. To me he always appeared much the same as in my earlier memories, but I had grown bigger and certainly much taller since that sinful morning at his fishpond, and I am sure that at no time did he recognise me in his church. Nevertheless, I felt a little nervous every time he looked in my direction.

At this point in my life, I was not yet nine, we, as a family, severed our connections with the Parish Church, although I hardly believe we could be considered proselytes, despite our subsequent affiliation to another society of worship.

The reason for this transfer, so far as I was able to ascertain from listening to the conversations of grown-ups, was that our local Parish Church seemed to hold itself remote from the hard, down-to-earth life endured by many members of its congregation. If there were absentees from the flock, whether it be due to illness or to any domestic problem, even over prolonged periods, the accusation was that the local dignitaries showed a remarkable lack of concern.

The Methodist fraternity on the other hand, whose place of worship lay at the bottom end of North Street, displayed a positively close interest in the welfare of their members, demonstrating both help and concern to any family or individual stricken by misfortune, and despite limited resources everything possible was done to ensure there was no shortage of essentials.

Upon these points — at my age then, and to this day — I have formed no opinion and have no comment to make upon the validity of such comparisons. All I remember is that I enjoyed attending the Methodist Chapel far more than I had the Parish Church.

For example, on a Sunday morning we children seldom joined the congregation in the chapel itself until very near the end of the service. The first and biggest part of our religious observance was conducted by a layman in a large adjoining room. Here we were always encouraged to question all that we did not understand. The subject matter gave us a wide scope and probably had the layman groping at times.

In that same room, every Wednesday evening, was held what was cheerfully called "Bright Hour". Actually it lasted nearer two hours, during which we played all sorts of competitive games. The evening was concluded with a couple of hymns and a prayer, and the building and its dedication, which had afforded us a fun-filled time, duly received a sincere deference from kids taught to care.

We enjoyed two or three tea parties in the course of a year, but the special one was just before Christmas when a number of toys was distributed among the less fortunate kids — a category in which I was included. These toys were not all new and had mostly been donated by children from more opulent homes, but they were more than welcomed by kids who had already learnt never to look a gift horse in the mouth.

This was a generous fraternity that indulged itself in more than one kind of religious service, yet without ceremony responded to a cry for help. And we did receive callers at Duck Lane, representatives of the Methodists, whenever we were thought to be in real need, or because sickness had struck at one or more of us.

I remained a disciple of that fraternity until shortly before I left school when, rightly or wrongly, my views had become much more secular.

CHAPTER
ELEVEN

Snake in the Grass

My early memories of shopping in Midhurst include queuing for two totally different sorts of food. Daily a queue was formed at the door of a cake shop in North Street. I joined this one often.

The cake shop sale was an early morning event, and took place before we went to school. Cakes that were left over from the previous day were sold off at tremendously reduced prices. Two pennyworth of stale cakes might include half a dozen or more assorted delicacies.

There were times that we lined up in vain. Either the shop had sold out on the previous day or the earlier arrivals at the head of the queue accounted for all that had been left over. The ladies who served in the shop usually tried to give everybody a near equal share, but try as they might they were not up to the Lord's standard when it came to doling out so little to so many.

The other queue was created every Friday evening by the arrival of a fish and chip van, which parked in a side lane just off West Street. My inclusion was irregular, depending upon current financial circumstances at home.

The arrival of the fish and chip van was in the nature of an impact, rather than a visit. Every nostril in the town was assailed, every taste bud titillated, and every nook and cranny in the area pervaded with the delicious aroma of fried fish.

The van was big and square looking, with a long, tin chimneystack set to one side in the roof. Winter or summer it was a popular sight in the town, save for a small minority who thought even the smell of fish and chips rather *infra dig*. Their objections were noted, but pushed aside by the more proletarian population of Midhurst. There was no rival business in the town so it did little if any harm to local trade.

Over the years there were many times that I went to bed feeling hungry — feel, being the operative word. I was perfectly well fed, but that mouth-watering aroma could stimulate the most insensitive of appetites.

This occurred frequently, certainly during the lean times when Father was out of work, after I had foolishly succumbed to curiosity and had gone along, without a penny in my pocket, just to look at the van and all the surrounding activity.

There were occasions that I sensibly kept right away, but such is the acuteness of young nostrils I could lie in bed, and even fall asleep, contemplating, in the mind's eye, a succulent piece of fried fish. I could clearly smell reality, although the van was stationed a couple of hundred yards away, with lots of houses in between. And all this, despite the active homemade wine arrayed at the foot of my bed; every uncorked bottle contributing to the piquant atmosphere which ever prevailed beneath the low ceiling of my sleeping quarters.

But there are many well remembered times when Mother would write out an order on a bit of paper, wrapping up the money inside, before sending me off on this most agreeable errand.

I loved to stand in the queue at the rear of the van and, although I was too short to observe much of what was going on in the back, I could hear the sizzle of fried ambrosia above the conversations of the grown-ups as they gossiped and waited their turn. And all the time I would be swallowing what seemed like pints of saliva in anticipation of things to come.

One evening as I stood in the queue, the man who was frying the fish and chips was also talking very seriously to a bunch of interested customers, some of whom were already eating his produce from the ever-popular newspaper wrapping, while others, like me, waited to be served. Except for the occasional "Oooh" and "Aaah" his audience remained very quiet until the end of the narrative.

It appeared that our host had not long before witnessed a fatal accident involving a motorcycle and a car, which he seemed very eager to describe. He dealt with every gory detail most enthusiastically. All agog, I listened intently, but today only one clear fact emerges from the shadows of time. I learned that evening the longest word I had ever heard: "instantaneously".

At home I had a very old dictionary, which someone had brought from school and, even as I tucked into my delicious supper, I looked up this long word. I went to bed wondering why the man had not simply said "instantly". Trust grown-ups to make things harder for themselves — as well as everyone else!

In those days many young children were called upon by their mothers to run small shopping errands, mostly upon arrival home from school. It was a reasonably safe undertaking, for normally there was little traffic about. I remember, as an exceedingly young lad, dribbling an old tennis ball down the centre of the entire length of North Street and the only thing I needed to avoid were the numerous deposits of horse manure. The Midhurst old folk had no problem in crossing the road either. What a difference half a century has made.

It seems to me, in those distant days, everything was purchased with varying numbers of pennyworths and, although there were two hundred and forty pennies in the pound, it took the average worker at least a couple of days to earn that pound.

I used to go to a grocer's shop in West Street to obtain Father's favourite brand of dark shag. It was contained in a large earthenware jar, which alongside others stood upon a high shelf. I must say that when the lid was lifted the smell of all that loose tobacco was quite delicious — almost nice enough to eat. Fortunately I was never tempted to that degree, which demands an experimental taste.

130

Parrot-fashion I would say, "Half an ounce of fourpenny shag, please." Although it was the cheapest of tobaccos it actually cost eightpence per ounce, but the men behind the counter knew me well enough and understood what I meant. For my part I loved the way in which they twisted a piece of paper around the tobacco, making a neat little parcel that looked extremely like an ice-cream cornet.

Another delightful aroma I always associate with that shop emanated then from a large hand-wound coffee grinder, which seemed to me at the time to be in almost constant use. Everytime I entered that establishment I must have had my nose in the air, rather like one of the Bisto Kids, enjoying a scent on the wafting breeze.

But despite all this it was "Half a pound of fourpenny marg", which constituted the very first sentence I learned by heart, simply because margarine was sold just around the corner at the International Stores: a short toddle, which did not necessitate crossing a single road. How well I recall the innumerable occasions when, as I made my way to the store and to the amusement of many a passer-by, I repeated quite audibly word for word my mother's instructions, including "And don't forget to say please." It seemed to me over the years that I was forever nipping round to the "Inter" for half a pound of fourpenny marg. It just goes to show how stable the price remained.

The highlight of the margarine mission lay not entirely in the delicious, multi-scented air, a feature of all grocer shops before the era of prepacked food. No, I found the greatest interest in watching a dollop of margarine, cut from a huge mass, being patted swiftly into a brick-like shape by a man wielding two flat pieces of wood. He then weighed the selected portion and wrapped it up in a veritable blur of fingers and greaseproof paper. Having watched this exhibition with never waning fascination I would then walk over to the cash desk and pay the lady occupant the sum of twopence.

Because Nan did a little domestic work here and there, she was able to afford the occasional cigarette. I was often prevailed upon to run the errand for some. Her order seldom differed, "Five Woodbines, please." Five Woodbines tucked side-by-side in a flimsy and partially open packet, cost twopence.

A pint of beer was fourpence (sixty pints to the pound!) and a haircut cost fourpence, too. Uncle Mossy often lamented that such high prices would never drop to their pre-war levels.

Two pennyworth of pieces from the butcher supplied enough meat for a family-size stew, and if garden produce happened to be in short supply, two pennyworth of "pot herbs" from the green grocer provided the vegetables.

There was one commodity for which the grocer would pay the customer. Glass jars, which had contained marmalade or jam, if collected on a large scale provided a modest moneymaking enterprise. For each one returned to the appropriate shop the grocer would pay one halfpenny.

I discovered at an early age that to take Father's truck on a trip to the local refuse tip could pay a handsome dividend. Through one such expedition I received two shillings from the cash desk at the International Store. That remained a personal record.

The International was the victim of a bit of juvenile skulduggery, which went on for quite a long time, and I am not saying that I was innocent.

If the big gate to the rear premises were open — and it nearly always was — it was possible to slip in from Duck Lane and grab a couple of empty jars from where they were stored in the yard ready for transport. These were then taken round to the front of the store where they were paid for once again. I do not recall who was caught in the act, but it ended the racket completely. From then on the returned jars were kept inside the building.

Throughout the warmer months there were other forms of errands to indulge in, unpaid commissions we kids loved to carry out. The raw material had to be gathered before homemade wine could be produced. This required the seasonal harvesting of nature's bounty, ranging from cowslips to elderberries, from sloes to dandelions. A dozen or so Duck Lane kids might join forces for this.

Then unusually the normal segregation of girls and boys at play disappeared entirely as both sexes seemed quite happy to get together in the interest of a common project. After all, no boy could sensibly boast that he was more proficient than his female counterpart when it came to picking flowers.

Most of the winemaking produce was to be found quite close to the town boundaries, but to find cowslips in the great profusion required a long walk — a round trip of at least five miles. We knew a spot, just above the fringe of some farmland on a lower ridge of the South Downs where cowslips grew in vast quantities. Every year we headed for this place, maybe half a dozen times, and we always returned heavily laden. Such trips usually included a picnic, so we carried food and drink on the outward jaunt and cowslips on the homeward trudge.

Handcarts and even old prams were sometimes trundled along and these helped to ease the burden on the long walk back — my truck was a bit too heavy to haul all that way. Even so, all wheeled transport had to be left behind as we ran out of beaten track and made our way for the last half mile or so over very rough and steeply rising ground. We toted a variety of receptacles: sacks and shopping bags being predominant. These would be filled with cowslips and relayed back to the parked vehicles over and over during the day.

There were many times, having reached the foot of the Downs when some of the older lads would — rather selfishly I now think — leave the girls and the younger boys hard at work gathering the flowers and set off for the higher ground. The climb to the top was very steep, but the magnificent view in all directions was compensation enough.

The Downs reached a height of about eight hundred feet at this point, and from the topmost crest on a clear day the coastline stretching from west of Portsmouth and the Isle of Wight to a region just short of Brighton could be seen. Looking inland over the parallel ridge of the North Downs, one might discern the far distant Leith Hill situated near Dorking — two-thirds of the way to Carshalton!

This part of the South Downs was then completely uncultivated, and the grass, which carpeted the seemingly limitless acres, was so springy it always felt like walking upon a well-sprung mattress. Sad it is to relate that most of this has long since been put to the plough as a direct result of the second world war, when all arable land was pressed into service.

Still encroaching the future, it was from these heights that I and many of my contemporaries were to watch, spellbound, the deadly fighting in the skies around, for these hills reached to the heavens, which would one day comprise the western sector of the Battle of Britain.

But all of this was yet to come and, happily, we played on.

One of the most popular, and silliest, of pranks we indulged in was in the nature of a contest. We would simply lie on our sides and allow ourselves to roll over and over down the longest and steepest slope in the vicinity until the feeling of giddiness and nausea compelled first one and then another of us to stop. The winner was, of course, the boy who rolled the furthest.

On a number of occasions I saw boys looking very shaken and pale-faced, especially after a particularly valiant effort, for it was not always possible to come to a halt when one so desired. Many were the lads who still felt sick a long time afterwards.

One boy of about twelve, who did not hail from Duck Lane but had been invited to join us, might well have lost his life through participating in this crazy pastime. If I remember rightly his name was David.

David, being new to the gang as well as the sport, was determined to win at all cost. Refusing to pull up where the slope levelled out and where most of us had already rolled to a halt, he went spinning on despite our warning cries. He disappeared over the edge of what we knew to be an almost vertical incline. It was the near precipitous face of a long disused chalk quarry — a drop of some two hundred feet.

We ran to the edge where, in horror, we watched his speedy descent. He no longer rolled; in an avalanche of crumbled chalk he was sliding and bumping his way along a very direct route to the foot of the Downs. We could see he was still conscious for he was desperately grabbing at the many tussocks, which clung to the chalk face; in fact he clawed and clutched at anything that might retard his progress, but gravity remained the master and on he went. The final part of his descent was fortunately less steep and far below us we saw him sprawl to a halt, seemingly lifeless, upon a grass-covered, gentle slope. He remained so still we thought he was dead.

136

More frightened for David than for ourselves, we clambered down the almost vertical face, which was a stupid thing to do, for as we did so we dislodged many pieces of chalk, some of which might well have struck the motionless figure below.

We were halfway down when we saw him stir and before we reached him he was sitting up. He had been badly winded, but that had righted itself, he was more concerned with all the cuts and fast developing bruises. But he was in one piece, which we thought was a miracle, and he was able to get to his feet without assistance. In the face of his moans and groans we rather callously pointed out that he had been very lucky, for he had rolled over the cliff edge at the one place where it was least steep below.

He was not over gratified when we declared him winner of the rolling contest, and later in the day he complained of an ache in his forearm. A day or so afterwards we learned that poor David had, indeed, sustained a broken arm. I still think he was lucky.

Oddly enough, those dutiful workers who remained on the lower slopes picking cowslips by the thousand did not protest much about the absence of the bigger lads. I suppose it was taken into account that the latter would, in the main, become the beasts of burden on the long trek home, pushing and carrying not only the harvest, but some of the smaller members of the company, whose little legs had given out on them. Usually, they rode high upon a fully laden pram or truck; if we were short of wheeled transport they received a pickaback ride.

I was only a toddler myself when, employed upon another such venture not so far from home, I received the biggest fright of my young life.

It was a gorgeous, early spring morning and a party of us was strung out along the hedgerow of a field, just above a sand quarry gouged out of land immediately adjacent to Midhurst railway station. We were all picking primroses, for the purpose of winemaking of course, when, as I extended my hand to gather a bunch of the said flowers, a very large adder wriggled across my wrist. To me, at the time, it was just a snake; it was later on in life that I realised it had been an adder.

I jumped to my feet, and very nearly out of my skin, and commenced screaming at the top of my tiny young voice. Everybody gathered around wondering what was wrong with me. I must have looked, and perhaps I was, demented. My sister, Daisy, could not placate me, although she did glean enough from my incoherent blubbering between screams to deduce that a snake had played a prominent part in the affair. This in turn unsettled her and she began to throw apprehensive glances all around.

In obvious response to my screams a man came hurrying towards us from a lonely little cottage at the far end of the meadow. Exchanging a few quick words with my sister he then, with much arm waving and foot stamping, pretended to chase the offending snake into an adjoining field.

138

He told my sister and the rest of the gang to carry on picking primroses and took me off to his little house. There his wife examined me from shoulders to fingertips and, finding nothing amiss, she wiped away my tears and offered me a glass of lemonade. I will never forget how my hands trembled as I accepted it.

I might well have been considered a very lucky young toddler, for an adder's bite in early spring can be particularly harmful. After hibernation, they are for a spell set upon sex rather than food. There is a strong chance that the glands, which secrete their venom, will be filled to capacity.

For the rest of my life my attitude towards snakes, venomous or not, remains unaltered. It may go its way; I will go mine. From that time on I have ever been alert to the possibility of there being a snake in the grass.

CHAPTER
TWELVE

Indoor Games

Most children at that time were familiar with every kind of indoor game. I refer not only to the games of chance, such as ludo or snakes and ladders, to which we were introduced at a very young age, but to the more thought demanding pastimes, such as dominoes, draughts and a wide variety of card games. These were eagerly taught by parents for long winter evenings spent without television, and in most cases without wireless in the home, required that the family had the ability to produce its own entertainment.

One of my fondest memories is that of beating Nan at draughts in a contest that was not rigged for me to win. In the early days she would take me on, using only six draughts against my twelve. Gradually, as I improved, this was increased to nine, but whatever the numerical odds in my favour I never won unless permitted, which was not very often; for as Nan explained, this was not the way to teach a person to play any kind of game. I must first learn to lose well and then, by my own endeavours, learn to win.

On the great occasion of my first genuine victory, we played twelve against twelve. I suppose I was seven or eight at the time and I knew in my own heart, besides Nan's many assurances, that the game had been truly played, and fairly won, by little me.

Dominoes was another popular game, and one which as a boy I thoroughly enjoyed. I was still a whipper-snapper, but I was a proficient player in all age groups of domino contenders.

My parents and most of my aunts and uncles were ardent whist players, so we children learned to play this game at an early age. Many a winter's evening was taken up with myself, Mother, Father and Daisy, all contesting keenly in a game, one parent and one child forming a partnership. At this stage Daisy was fast becoming a very good player. She had not yet left school, although that milestone of her life was not very far away, when Father invited her to try her hand at a real whist drive partnership. At first she demurred, but after much coaxing she finally agreed to go along with him, and early one dark evening off they went together.

I was allowed to stay up late that evening. Cecil had been put to bed, Marjorie was asleep in her pram, and Mother and I sat by the fireside and talked, and read, and waited. The evening dragged on and then, soon after nine-thirty, the front door opened and Daisy entered the little room, looking terribly sad. Father followed with a stern expression upon his face.

"Well?" queried Mother with a bit of a frown.

"She was utterly useless," growled Father, "You'd 'ave thought she'd never played the game before. Utterly useless."

141

Mother stared incredulously. "What went wrong? She plays well enough here. Did she suffer with nerves or something?"

She directed the last question at poor Daisy rather more than Father, but it was he that answered. He began to smile broadly, his weather-beaten face crinkled merrily in the glow of the oil lamp as he produced a black handbag with slow deliberation from behind his back.

"First time! First prize!" he exclaimed triumphantly. "She got the cards an' she knew what to do with 'em."

I shall never forget the change of expression on Mother's face, and as for me I was near to tears of both relief and joy. Father, too, had won a prize, but for the life of me I cannot recall what it was. We were all so happy for Daisy that everything else was overshadowed.

Such are the many well remembered incidentals, etched for all time in my mind, possibly because they were products of a simpler age — maybe happily — just short of these present days of easy to come by, taken for granted, radio and television.

We, the poorer children of that era, were quick to learn that very little was easily come by. Consequently, we were ever on the alert for an opportunity to earn a few pence, and I was, like most of the Midhurst kids, ready to win a few pence whenever the chance arose — and it did just once a year.

Goodwood racecourse is situated some six or seven miles from Midhurst. Here a four-day flat race meeting was held annually, beginning on the last Tuesday of July. The local schools at that time broke up for the summer holidays just before Goodwood Week, as it was popularly known, and, luckily for me, just before I left for my annual holiday at Carshalton. It was most fortunate, for the monetary proceeds acquired throughout the four days of Goodwood easily paid for my return fare by train, the surplus coming in useful as pocket-money.

In those days the traffic moved less quickly and the main stream of vehicles bound for Goodwood passed through Midhurst. Since two lines of traffic converged at Midhurst and there was a single route to the racecourse, the town and the approaches would often be snarled up with vehicles of all descriptions, from charabancs to London taxis.

Children of all ages gathered in small groups along the route in and out of the town. It was seldom advantageous to stand alone. A good place was the pull-in at a public house; there again, advantage was lost if there were too many children around.

Wherever the location, all we had to do initially was to yell, repeatedly, "Throw out yer rusty coppers."

Over the years this had provided a source of amusement to the occupants of the vehicles as, bumper to bumper, the stream of traffic snarled its way in and out of the town. They responded to our vociferous plea, especially the people in the charabancs, by throwing out handfuls of small change, mostly coppers, even farthings, but occasionally there would appear a flash of silver in the air. With or without the silver, the cascade

143

of wealth at once transformed a group of seemingly friendly children into a heap of clawing, pinching, stamping, grabbing individuals, much to the great amusement of the motorized audience.

I have heard it said that we scrambled for money: a euphemism, I must say! Broken and discoloured nails, with swollen black blobs, which appeared beneath the skin of our sore fingers, were the scars we proudly bore, for many a misdirected foot would stamp down upon an unprotected hand instead of upon the intended coin. But we were all happy about it, for where else were we to obtain such an amount of money in such a short time?

It was not only children who took advantage of this annual benevolence. The local hospital and the workhouse, both situated on the same stretch of road in the neighbouring parish of Easebourne, also participated in collecting "rusty coppers", but their way was more efficient and far less violent. They identified themselves with signboards and laid out large sheets alongside the road into which their benefactors might toss their gifts. I recall many occasions that I saw the silvery glint of superior denominations among the heaps of coppers.

This led to ideas. A bunch of Duck Lane kids, including me, tried it on one day by painting a red cross on a piece of cardboard and laying out a moth-eaten sheet. A policeman soon intervened and that was the end of that — until the evening.

The whole thing was a twice-daily affair and the race goers began their return trip in the early evening. Again we took along our red-cross sign and laid out our sheet.

This time it was an AA man who intervened. He was much more belligerent than the policeman. Our signboard was torn to shreds and the few coppers that lay upon the sheet were confiscated, and he certainly gave us a dressing down, full of awful threats. For a long time afterwards I regarded AA men with a feeling of nervousness.

Another source of annual income, although nothing like so lucrative, presented itself in the early autumn. A local corn merchant, who also ran a pig farm, would give the swine a treat by feeding them acorns. He paid the sum of fourpence for a bushel, which we kids thought quite generous. On school days, early mornings and later afternoons were reserved for gathering acorns. It was usual for two or three of us to work together, sharing a sack or, if the terrain permitted, a hand-truck. We made sure that the location of any prolific source remained a jealously guarded secret. The red-herring schemes we devised in order to conceal our true destinations were sometimes quite elaborate, sometimes hilarious, and most times ineffectual.

One example that comes easily to mind took place on a cold, drizzling early evening. My old pal Dick and I, noting that a rival team were preparing to set out, decided to leave the town on a northerly course whereas we needed to go south to reach our secret source, which we had discovered during a ramble on the previous Sunday.

Moving out into the country, and using all the available cover, we changed direction and by a long

145

roundabout route finally came upon our destination, only to find the rival team clearing up the remains of a bountiful harvest, the bulk of which was heaped in their hand-cart. And we were wet through, too!

But we did not always lose out, and a good year for acorns would provide ample funds for fireworks on the fifth of November, with a little left over for Christmas presents.

To gather acorns early on a frosty or rain-swept morning is not the most comfortable of pastimes, but it was a way to earn money and we accepted the hardships without question. Even as our fathers did, when they were not fortunate enough to find employment.

I was not quite nine when Father was lucky enough to find work at a building site in Singleton, about six miles away. Unless he was able to get a lift en route, he walked both ways. At that time there was not a lot of transport about on an average day, so Father, small of stature but tough and wiry, must certainly have worn out a whole heap of hobnails.

It was the day before I was due to leave for my summer holiday at Carshalton that, early in the morning, I accompanied my father on his walk to Singleton. Overnight I had pleaded to be allowed to go to work with him, and had been almost in tears before, nodding his head as though to say "You'll learn", Father finally agreed.

The outward journey did not worry me at all and I arrived at our destination feeling as full of life as when leaving home. Father repeatedly told me not to run about too much during the day, for the weather was too warm and I would need a reserve of energy for the walk home. I did not adhere to this good advice and by late afternoon the thought of the long trek to Midhurst was, even in my young mind, daunting. Even so, I reasoned, if Father could work all day using a grub axe and shovel and then walk home with a firm step, I ought to make it easily.

We had not walked far, although we had climbed a long steep hill, when my little legs began their silent protest. Father was just about to give me a pickaback ride, when a motorcycle combination overtook us and pulled up. "Want a lift, Jack?" asked the rider.

Father's face reflected the relief I felt, for my feet were already lead weights. I was placed in the sidecar and Father rode pillion. It was my first experience with a motorbike and I loved every moment of it, wishing, quite contrary to my inclinations a short while before, that Midhurst were a far more distant place.

Whether or not my father was fortunate enough to get many lifts like that I do not know, but remembering the prospect of that walk home I never once asked to accompany him again. It did not occur to me at the time, but the outlook must have been pretty bleak for him when it poured with rain.

CHAPTER
THIRTEEN

Top of the Class

By this time the hovels in Duck Lane had been condemned as being unfit for human habitation. The RSPCA could be the only objectors, for what would all those poor little creatures feed upon once we had left. The snag was that there was no alternative accommodation for us, so that we continued to dwell therein.

I was nine years old and having, once again, returned from my annual holiday at Carshalton, I was back at school for the autumn term. Miss Whittington was my teacher. She was highly skilled at rapping the knuckles of fractious pupils with a foot long ruler that moved at the speed of light. In all other respects she was a homely, rather endearing, middle-aged lady. I think I was one of her favourites and I know, because she told me years after I had left school, that she rated me highly as a student. But my ears continued to plague me and, although I remained a keen and promising scholar, my attendance was very erratic throughout the whole of the term.

Miss Whittington could do absolutely nothing about my accursed affliction, but she always extended a great measure of sympathy towards me, and in the course of the usual boisterous games, which took place on the playground, she did at times become over-protective. If she happened to be present, she would upbraid any boy who dared give me as much as a belligerent glare. "No fighting with Ron," she would say, "Remember the condition of his ears." At the time I did not quite appreciate her motives, and I fervently hoped I would not be considered a coward by my contemporaries.

Most unexpectedly, I gained top place at the end of term examination. My parents, especially Mother who was more scholastically minded, were tremendously pleased with the glowing report written by Miss Whittington; the more so in the light of my poor attendance record, which, alas, grew even worse after the Christmas holidays.

Before my life was totally interrupted by ear-trouble, I won one more small prize. We did no homework in those days, but once in a while Miss Whittington would set us a problem to be solved in our own time. This particular question I well recall, and how an afterthought won the day for me. The problem was to calculate exactly how many minutes long was Great Britain's participation in the 1914–18 war. It was simple enough to establish the precise time of its commencement, and the exact moment of the armistice was recalled every year even in tiny Midhurst as we stood in a two minute silence, preceded and concluded by a distant explosion, which symbolized the sound of cannon fire.

Long sets of figures were entailed in arriving at an answer, but, with care, it was fairly straightforward. Miss Whittington had put up a prize of sixpence, to be shared in the event of more than one correct answer.

I won the prize outright, but only just. At a late hour I suddenly realised that 1916, being "divisible by four" with no remainder, was a leap year. I promptly added 1,440 minutes to my original answer. Incredibly, only one other person had taken this into account. Fortunately for me, his arithmetic was faulty.

The new year progressed and saw me in dire trouble with my left ear. There would be a discharge from a burst abscess even as another was painfully forming. Earache was almost incessant, dragging me down both mentally and physically.

Finally, in early March, a visiting specialist at the local cottage hospital diagnosed mastoiditis, and almost immediately I underwent a major operation. Again, so far as I was concerned, it was the chloroform that was to be feared most of all.

After spending ten days in hospital, I became a frequent visitor as an outpatient. My entire head was swathed in a veritable turban of bandages, which, when required was deftly removed by a nurse. She would then steadily draw, inch by inch, a twine of yellow gauze from out of the cavity, which existed behind my left ear.

This exercise I observed out of the corner of my eye, and the nurse's hand reminded me of a black bird (they are so good at it) pulling a worm very carefully, so as not to snap it, from its hole in the ground. But I must admit I had never seen a worm as long and as fat as those early twines of yellow gauze. After inspection the same type of dressing was renewed.

Like most folk I had upon more than one occasion been called empty-headed, and during those first few post-operative days I thought there might be some truth in this assertion, in view of the amount of stuffing my head was able to accommodate. But as time progressed the volume of dressing was steadily reduced until the wound healed over altogether.

The great danger, according to the specialist who operated upon me, was meningitis, but I suffered no secondary infections and made a speedy recovery. Although over the years to follow I continued to have trouble with the left ear, it was never to the extent preceding that operation.

Fully recovered I applied successfully for my first real job.

CHAPTER
FOURTEEN

My First Job

I became "Boots" at Lyndale School, a seat of learning for young girls run by a neat, rather Victorian-looking lady called Miss Westcott.

Once a large private house, the building had a narrow frontage in Church Hill, not far from Aunt Daisy's abode. It provided accommodation for a number of boarders who in turn provided me with my primary task: cleaning shoes.

At the rear of the house was a spacious vegetable garden. At its furthest extremity it was bordered by a stone wall, roughly twenty yards long and about five feet high. On the other side of the wall, some twelve feet below, was a corresponding length of Duck Lane. Seen from here this lofty wall abutted the front corner of the row of seven hovels and ran alongside the lane to a point just short of its junction with West Street. The close proximity of both garden and wall to Duck Lane was to prove a very favourable factor in a subsequent venture. But of that, more anon.

Every weekday I hurried from my own school and arrived at Lyndale School soon after four o'clock. My first and principal job was to clean, most fastidiously, a motley array of feminine footwear, ranging from gym shoes to heavy brogues, with the current weather conditions dictating the predominant type of footwear. There were seldom more than fifteen pairs of shoes at any one time. I am at a loss as to how many girls attended the school. Considerably more than fifteen, I would guess, but I never once saw all the pupils together. I worked, for the most part, in the kitchen quarters at the extreme rear of the house.

I had many other duties, such as washing up enormous quantities of crockery and culinary utensils. I also cleaned and sharpened cutlery, using an old hand-cranked machine.

There was a part-time gardener, whom I rarely met, but there were plenty of occasions when I assisted him in his absence. Miss Westcott often asked me to do a little weeding and grass-cutting, although there were no lawns, only grass pathways that stretched across the garden here and there giving access to various plots. In the autumn I was required to sweep up leaves and make a bonfire of them, which was much more fun.

For a nine years old boy the remuneration for my work was extremely good, sixpence an hour, which might be appreciated the more when one considers that the hourly rate for an adult labourer was no more than tenpence, or elevenpence at the most.

I saw it as a penny for every ten minutes, and made out my own timesheet on a calendar, which hung on the kitchen wall. I made certain, even if I were forced to hide in the lavatory or skulk for a few minutes in a remote corner of the establishment, that my duties were

153

completed and recorded in cycles of ten minutes: never a minute short (my advantage) and never a minute over (Miss Westcott's advantage).

Depending upon the amount of work required, I generally put in a little more than an hour in the late afternoons, and two to three hours on a Saturday morning. In a busy week I might earn as much as five shillings (25p). This was more than the weekly rent for our hovel in Duck Lane, so that it will be acknowledged that I was doing quite well.

My old pursuits, such as the coke conveyance business, had been left to younger associates, and as for gathering acorns it was only seasonal, and it was cold to the fingers on a frosty morning. Comparing it with my present situation, I found I had no regrets over the loss of that job at all. Furthermore, my present employment permitted me to continue my annual holidays at Carshalton, since my place of work was closed for that same period.

This aspect was convenient in more than one way: upon my return from holiday I began to earn money at the usual rate, unlike the rewards of the coke business, which had to be built up every year in just the same way as after an enforced absence due to ear trouble.

Mother took only sixpence a week from me, which was put in a club of some sort and provided me with clothing. If I remember rightly, it was paid to a very pleasant tallyman by the name of Mr. East who used to call regularly at several homes in Duck Lane, carrying his wares in suitcases tied to the rear carrier of his bicycle.

My weekly pocket money was more than adequate and I was made to put a little aside for holidays and Christmas. Already I was less of a drag upon the family finances. At times I felt quite grown up.

At Lyndale School on Saturday mornings I did all sorts of odd jobs, including one particular task which took me to the front of the house but only at cellar level. Every week I was called upon to clear up the areas immediately beneath two iron gratings, which were set apart by just a few feet in the public footpath, in front of the house hard to the wall. These had at one time been used when coal was delivered to the cellar.

Long disused, they served merely to illuminate the cellar with narrow shafts of daylight, which daily, imperceptibly, moved along the floor from west to east. It seemed to me that trapped beneath their bars was all the refuse, especially paper, that would otherwise have littered Church Hill.

Innate propriety forbids me to expound upon the considerable variations, both in colour and design, of a particular item of lingerie observed from this below-the-pavement vista, inadvertently, I hasten to add. It was quite educational to a growing lad.

It was in this cellar that I came upon the biggest toad I ever saw. Miss Westcott had warned me to be careful where I placed my feet in the darker quarters of the basement; not in my interest, but in those of the toad, for she had seen the creature on a number of occasions and had, once, all but trodden upon it.

155

One Saturday morning I came face to face with it (that is a slight exaggeration; it was not quite that tall) but there it sat motionless looking larger than life-size, sleepy-eyed and apparently unafraid in a pool of sunlight beaming in through one of the gratings. As I sidled, a little nervously, towards it I could see that the toad was not at all motionless; the corpulent body was clearly pulsating heavily beneath its rough, wart-blemished skin. This observation, coupled with a searching gaze at its rather stupid-looking face, gave rise to my first impression that I was regarding a singularly unattractive presence. My ensuing attachment to this creature most certainly did not begin with love at first sight.

Yet I declare, as the weeks passed by, there developed a certain affinity between us. For my part, I was acutely disappointed whenever I visited the cellar and failed to meet up with my companion of the damp and dark. There were times, mostly in the winter, that I carried a lighted candle, but even so if he did not make his presence known I could never find him. I use the masculine pronoun, but I never established its sex.

I think Tommy Toad, for so had I named it, used to sleep away a lot of time in one or another of the many deep crevices afforded by the rough masonry of the basement walls. But there were delightful occasions when Tommy would approach from the privacy of a dark corner, I swear, just to greet me. Although he appeared to be quite nonchalant as I stroked his dry, coarse shoulders, I am certain he really loved it, and he would even permit me to tickle him under his

156

ponderously jowled chin. Miss Westcott conceded that, despite such an unlikely association, she could see we were the best of friends.

One morning, a day or so before I was due to leave for my holiday at Carshalton, I said my farewells to Tommy, explaining my forthcoming absence and assuring him that I would see him again in September.

We were never to meet again.

It transpired that, quite near the end of my vacation, a young friend of the gardener, a boy a little older than I, had occasion to visit the cellar. It would seem that he was a bit of a "do-gooder" for, no doubt with well-disposed intention, he transported Tommy to the vegetable garden. I imagine the boy considered the creature would be happier outdoors.

The day before my return from Carshalton poor Tommy was found dead, lacerated terribly by an unknown animal, but by a cat, a dog, or what? No one had decided.

I think it was Miss Westcott herself who had interred Tommy's mutilated remains in a disused corner of the raspberry bed. She had marked the grave with a tiny wooden cross, and that little plot of land was extremely well tended, to my certain knowledge, until the day I finally left the job.

Soon after Tommy's death I fell in love for the first time with one of the girl boarders whose name, if I remember rightly, was June. I flatter myself that my interest was reciprocated.

The girls were not normally allowed in the kitchen quarters, but June repeatedly omitted to leave her shoes at a selected place in one of the corridors. It was the practice for a female member of the staff to collect them and bring them to the kitchen, where they were lined up along a worktop in readiness for me to clean.

More often than not I was alone in the kitchen when I polished away at all this footwear. June would pay me a visit, always carrying the pair of shoes she had purposely forgotten to leave out. She was a little older than I, and very pretty. She had the most wonderfully cultured voice to which I listened spellbound. She told me all about her mummy and daddy, their big house and garden, and even a pony that she rode, apparently, with a fair degree of skill. To this day I refuse to think she was bragging, for that was not in her nature, nor did she, even unwittingly, humiliate me in any way. She simply liked to talk to me, but equally she liked to listen. When I told her where I lived and of all the surrounding circumstances she shook her head, not in disbelief, but in sympathy, and she professed an understanding of all the things I hoped she would never experience.

Our innocent encounters continued for many months, chiefly through the indulgence of a servant, a teenage girl who winked at our liaison very kindly and often warned June of the approach of Miss Westcott.

It was just before the Christmas holidays that June, bringing along a perfectly clean pair of shoes, told me that she would have to wish me a happy Christmas early, for she was leaving for home the next day.

She leaned forward and, for the very first time, kissed me full on the lips. I am not sure just what sort of blissful disposition might have been engendered by that intimate, physical contact, but it was not the reason for my heart missing several beats at that very moment. Indeed not, for over June's slender shoulder I perceived Miss Westcott, standing in the open doorway and looking aghast.

To me she said very little, muttering in my direction something about being surprised and putting a stop to it, but her voice was a whiplash as she ordered June to her dormitory. I learned afterwards the poor girl was berated most severely and even threatened with expulsion.

Sadly, I never again conversed with June. Sometimes I would catch sight of her in the front quarters of the building, but this was usually through a window from which on rare occasions, she managed a furtive wave. There were times that we passed each other by, sometimes in the courtyard, sometimes in the garden. We would exchange both a smile and a greeting, but never once did we stop to talk.

My first love affair was over, but to be perfectly truthful I missed poor Tommy far more than I did June.

As I have mentioned, I was never keen on gardening, but on Saturday mornings I spent quite a lot of time in the garden of Lyndale School. I found it to be a most gratifying occupation — at a penny for every ten minutes.

159

In the northwest corner of the garden there was a very healthy plantation of fruit bushes. It included gooseberries, red and black currants, and, in a large plot protected by netting, strawberries and the raspberries, which grew near Tommy's grave. I never knew the gardener's secret, but every year this part of the garden seemed to yield a bounteous harvest.

At the appropriate time, armed with a couple of trug baskets, it was my mouth-watering duty to pick whichever fruit was ready for gathering and to take it to the kitchen. Usually, under the supervision of Miss Westcott, it was preserved, immediately or later, depending upon the process selected.

Whenever I went fruit picking it was seldom under supervision, Miss Westcott being wise enough to know that I would initially have my fill of whatever I fancied, before the novelty wore off. With a diminished appetite for fruit, my wavering interest in harvesting was supported only by the ulterior motive of earning money.

As boys go, I had always been considered to be trustworthy and honest by all who knew me well. But there is generally a flaw in the most virtuous character and, since I hardly qualified for inclusion in that category, there was in mine a gaping hole through which temptation flowed, surging and urging me to take advantage of the situation and to go "scrumping". I began to plot.

The fact that by so doing I would abuse a trust did not occur to me. All is fair in the "scrumping" world. My young pals in Duck Lane rarely ate fresh fruit in the abundance I would be able to provide. If we received any at all from a shop it was usually over-ripe and referred to as speckled fruit, being cheaper to purchase. But it was certainly less palatable than fresh fruit, being mostly badly bruised and half eaten by wasps and flies. Even a hungry child is selective, if there be a choice.

Strangely enough, I stood to gain nothing from this venture, which as yet was but a burgeoning idea, except the admiration of my pals. But I did feel that the kids of the lane had as much right to fresh fruit as any of the more pampered and privileged girls at the school, including June. As I saw it Miss Westcott was the Sheriff of Nottingham and I was Robin Hood.

Before I left home for work I would fold up a few brown paper bags, easily acquired in those days since almost every kind of shop used them, and these I would hide about my person. Next I concealed a reel of thin string, some twenty feet in length. I would take my leave of Duck Lane, having usually delegated my trusty young friend, Dick, as commander-in-chief of all operations at the base of the high wall, which ran towards West Street.

My rôle, on the other side of the wall, was to fill a paper bag with whatever fruit I was picking at the time and, having tied it securely at the neck, lower it by means of the reel of string to Dick who would be waiting in the lane below. One further improvisation had to be made. The height of the wall on my side in the fruit growing area was a little more than five feet, way above my head and too tall for me to reach over.

A forked stick was the answer. It needed to be no more than two feet long, quite unobtrusive when placed beneath a bush. Its function was to lift the bag over the top of the wall. By passing the string through the cleft in the stick and keeping the line taut I was able to hold the neck of the bag in the cleft until I had pushed the stick far enough over the wall to enable me to run out the line and so gently lower the bag. It had to be done gently for the fruit being 'scrumped' would make such a giveaway mess if treated roughly.

There was also a signal code. Just as soon as Dick saw the bag appear at the top of the wall he would give a single low whistle. This told me to lower away, there being nobody representing trouble in the lane. Two shrill notes warned me to stop: alien approaching.

If all was clear the operation took only a minute or so to complete; it needed no more than seconds for Dick to detach the bag and for me to retrieve the line. But three or four full bags was about the limit for any one day's undertaking, and I had to work fast to accomplish that for, although Miss Westcott was in no way a slave driver, she did expect the trug baskets to be filled and brought to the kitchen in reasonable periods of time.

Dick always doled out the fruit to the kids of the lane, giving himself a fair share, of course, and it is a wonder to this day that I was never denounced; not perhaps by the children, but by their parents who surely must have known or guessed something about our venture. Telltale stains on tiny hands would alone have alerted suspicions.

But there was one occasion that I was very nearly caught out by Miss Westcott herself. Because I knew I was fairly well concealed from the windows of the school by the very bushes I was employed upon, and by a tracery of branches that stemmed from a small apple tree, I suppose I had grown rather careless.

Anyone approaching me from the house had to cross a wide stretch of open ground. The reason I did not see the advance of my boss, despite the fact that at the time I was engaged upon my nefarious endeavours, was obviously that I did not throw enough glances over my shoulder.

Had Miss Westcott arrived seconds earlier she would have certainly caught me red-handed. Dick had just detached the loot — blackcurrants I well remember — and I was about to pull the string back over the wall when a slight movement caught the corner of my eye and I was suddenly aware that Miss Westcott was peering at me through, fortunately, a blackcurrant bush of tall and thick proportions.

I had to let Dick know that I was no longer alone, just in case he tugged at the string again, which was the signal for me to haul it in. A movement like that would surely have caught her eye. I was standing, partially blocking her view, but I was acutely aware that just behind and above me was a piece of string hanging over that greyish stone wall, as vivid as a white line on a blackboard. "Crumbs, Miss," I blurted out loudly, "You didn't 'alf make me jump." I silently prayed that Dick had heard my voice.

Miss Westcott merely smiled, remarking that she had been waiting for some blackcurrants, and so saying she picked up a basket, which I had filled some time earlier and turned away, leaving me to the garden and the tail end of a cold sweat. There was never lack of caution after that.

It was, without doubt, a very foolish enterprise, for I only gained childish adulation and had everything to lose. The only redeeming feature might be that the Duck Lane kids received a lot more vitamin C than they would otherwise. But that consideration did not enter my thoughts at the time. The scrumping scheme was carried out purely in the interest of sheer excitement.

CHAPTER
FIFTEEN

Fumigated

At school during that summer I did very well, coming top of the class in the end of term examination. I enjoyed my holiday at Carshalton as usual and returned, aged ten, to a new classroom and a new teacher, Miss McClellan.

Every full-blooded youngster held a place in his or her heart for Miss Mac. Nothing school-marmish about her, she was — as the best romantic novels put it — young, dark and attractive. The fact that I do not recall the colour of her eyes is rather strange, for I remember so well that when she smiled they sparkled like sunlight upon rippling waters; an observation mentally recorded at the time, not an impression exaggerated by time.

She travelled daily from Wisborough Green, a village some twelve miles away, and every morning she parked her motorcar in a garage just above the turning into Petersfield Road. From here she walked to the school and if we happened to be on the spot at the right moment we young gallants deemed it an honourable pleasure to escort her. How clearly I recall swinging round the corner into Petersfield Road almost every morning, my eyes searching for the number plate JG

5270 in the gloomy interior of the garage, the big sliding doors of which were usually partially open.

But even ultra-young blades must face up to hard facts at times and I was not quite so enamoured with Miss Mac upon the occasion she introduced me to the intricacies of converting fractions to decimals. This was but a temporary disenchantment, and all was forgiven the very moment she acquainted me with that wonderful classic, Lorna Doone. How I lapped it up, and to this day it remains with me a great favourite in the realms of fiction, the mention of which ever reminds me of a great favourite from the realms of reality.

By this time my brother, Cecil, had become a schoolboy. Because of his poor health he had been a late starter and, although it might be remembered that I had been trained in the art of fisticuffs with a view to taking care of him — still a priority in Father's doctrine — he usually toddled to and from school under the protective custody of our eldest sister, Daisy. This would continue for only a few more months, for Daisy was fast approaching school leaving age.

Towards Christmas I began to suffer repeatedly with my ears. This time it was the right one that was by far the more troublesome.

Even when the condition permitted me to attend school, there were several Wednesday afternoons that, because of this affliction, I was compelled to miss my beloved game of football. I would have to sit quietly in the classroom, usually reading, while the rest of the boys were marched across the road by Mr. Purser to a field that lay near the junction of June Lane with Petersfield Road.

Here, according to size and ability, the lads were selected to play in one of two matches. The lower part of the field was consigned to the "little-uns", and here the pitch was unmarked and thin sticks were in use as goal posts. The top half of the field boasted a marked pitch with real goal posts, although there were no nets. This, of course, was reserved for the "big-uns".

Mr. Purser was referee for the senior game, and any lad who was old enough and big enough to ensure a certain authority — yet, as in most cases, was not much good at playing football himself — could volunteer to officiate the junior match.

At the same time the senior girls were marched up a steep hill at the rear of the school to a clearing on the common, which served as a netball pitch. Here, as well as being arbiter, Miss Mac very often joined in; ostensibly no doubt to demonstrate, but I know she loved the game.

The junior girls played netball on the silver-sand surface of the playground. It was not too bad after a recent rainfall; otherwise it was extremely dusty, particularly in a breeze. Miss Whittington presided here, usually from the sideline.

The senior football pitch was laid out on an incline that would shame the famous Yeovil slope, but at least the grass was always close-cropped due to the tenancy of a plump, brown pony, which I believe belonged to a school governor who lived near by.

Beyond the pitch, over a slight ridge at the far end of the field bounded with both wire netting and barbed wire, were the school garden plots. Here labour, under the guise of tuition, was supervised every Monday afternoon by a local professional gardener.

The lower football pitch, and indeed quite a lot of the ground above it, could not be easily observed from the furthest side of the garden, for here the land fell away sharply. If our mentor was engaged in this area and we were not, many were the times the more daring of us would sneak away from the garden with the object of mounting and riding the little pony; much more entertaining than gardening.

It certainly promoted in me a tremendous admiration for all those Hollywood redskins who rode bareback and at the same time brandished weapons above their heads. True we had no reins to grasp, but not one of us stayed mounted for more than a few seconds. I feel the pony cared little for us or our intentions.

As in the case of football, depending upon the current condition of my ears, gardening was at times considered too strenuous for me and I would remain behind in the classroom on a Monday afternoon. I seldom minded this for I had little interest in gardening. Missing a likely chance to ride, or at least attempt to ride, that uncompromising pony was my only regret.

In summer the same arrangements held, but naturally the winter games gave way to stoolball and cricket.

★   ★   ★

Just before we were due to break up for the Christmas holiday, an infection in my right ear flared up savagely. Although I took no part in the end of term examination Miss Mac wrote a comforting report on my academic progress. It also included the sincere hope that I would soon be rid of this persistent ear problem. It was a kind wish, but sadly it was not prophetic.

My school attendance after the holiday was of such a sporadic nature it became farcical. I was suffering abominably with the right ear. The local doctors tried all kinds of liquid and powder applications; the eardrum was deliberately perforated, but in the end the specialist's report indicated mastoiditis. An operation was immediately arranged.

It took place around the middle of March, again at the local cottage hospital, and this time the condition was more serious than it had been in the left ear a year earlier. Nevertheless, I recovered in much the same time and, once more, my pet aversion was the chloroform.

My head was still swathed in bandages when misfortune struck the family again. Cecil who was just beginning to outgrow his congenital stomach weakness went down with scarlet fever. He was very ill and was promptly whisked off to the isolation hospital at Brighton. I did not see him for an exceedingly long spell, for there in that same hospital having recovered from scarlet fever he contracted diphtheria, which very nearly finished him. But I run ahead of my story.

At the time of poor Cecil's departure in the ambulance it was decided, by some power of authority, that our hovel in Duck Lane must be fumigated. The windows, the doors and even the keyholes were to be sealed up for the duration of a whole morning and afternoon. Special candles were to be lit in each room, giving off fumes of sulphur dioxide. I did not feel much concerned about the impending fate of the colony of fleas, which existed stubbornly behind the layers of wallpaper and bulging plaster, nor did I fret about the threat of extinction for a multitude of spiders. I had ever felt indifference with regard to them. I did feel just a little bit sorry for the black beetles, for they had provided such good sport in the past, and were still good for a bit of fun when neither of my parents was around.

A date was arranged, it turned out to be one of those April mornings, which unexpectedly brings in its wake an icy cold, God-forsaken day. As the hours passed, the weather worsened. A bitterly cold northeaster, bringing along heavy showers of wet snow, blew continuously throughout the day. And there we were, cast out like lepers of old. Father was at work, so there were just the four of us: my mother, two sisters and myself. It was no fun for me, or the family. No one dared to take us in, especially those with children, for fear of infection. In a pitiable attempt to keep warm, we began to tramp the streets of Midhurst.

We had been advised to remain clear of close contact with all others throughout the day. In view of the prevailing conditions we might well have sought shelter

170

at Nan's house if only she were not taking care of two young cousins of mine who were down from London because their mother was detained in hospital for a spell. Neither of these children had suffered scarlet fever; the risk of infecting them was too great.

Doggedly we walked the streets and lanes avoiding the bitter blasts that funnelled from the northeast as best we could. From a respectful distance we acknowledged the many words and gestures of sympathy from almost everybody who saw us, for Midhurst was a very small place and most folk knew us and of our predicament, but could do nothing to help.

My principal duty that abominable day was to carry the basket containing our sustenance for the entire duration, mainly sandwiches. I had no gloves and throughout those long cold hours I periodically transferred the basket from one arm to the other, thrusting the hand that had most recently been exposed to the elements deep into my trouser pocket.

Marjorie was not yet four, so for quite a lot of the time she was carried alternately by Mother and Daisy. Marjorie was a bonny young girl, easily the healthiest child of our family, and right through her childhood she was to remain that way. But upon that bleak, snowy April day she was surely the hardest hit. Too young to appreciate the value of exercise, she cried miserably as she tried desperately to snuggle impossibly closer to Daisy or Mother in an attempt to seek warmth. A warmth that surely became increasingly harder to find even as morning reached noon.

As for me, besides my hands, I was sorely troubled by my knees, which were chapping badly in the wet and stinging wind; short trousers are not to be recommended for this kind of weather. But at least my head and ears remained dry and cosy. This was due to the turban of bandages, on the top of which was perched a large and fairly new peaked-cap (actually it was on loan from Father), which was secured in defiance of the strongest squall by a couple of safety-pins: an absurd looking headdress, but none the less effective.

I suspect the weather had turned surprisingly foul at very short notice for I am convinced that, had Father envisaged a day remotely like this, overnight he would have suggested what I then, that icy midday, thought to be a brilliant inspiration on Mother's part. We would go along to the building site where he worked.

Father was currently employed upon the construction of a swimming pools sited well to the rear of the local Grammar School, which was situated at the lower end of North Street. Mother was mindful of the layout since some time earlier Father had given her a conducted tour of the place. She remembered that on site there was a small, portable mess-hut and outside the open doorway there stood a big, iron brazier. She would not seek admission to the hut for she was aware that some of the workmen had children of their own and we must not run the risk of contaminating them, but she was sure we would be allowed to warm ourselves by the fire.

As we entered the site a man in a ragged overcoat greeted us and introduced himself as foreman. He told us to stand round the fire. We all but ran towards it. I was familiar at an early age of the association of hell with fire, brimstone and all, but as we gathered in its heat I was certain that this coke-stoked, red-hot brazier was no less than a direct gift from heaven itself. Mercifully we began to thaw.

The foreman told us that Father was somewhere in the town looking for us. He had left the site several times in the morning hoping that he might find us and shepherd us to this very place. Presently Father arrived on the scene. He looked rather more relieved than surprised for he had been told that his little flock were seen entering the narrow lane alongside the Vicar's garden. At once he knew we were making for the building site.

With several bricks and a couple of planks Father soon provided sitting accommodation, but we remained outside and we were still exposed to most of the rigours of that filthy day. It was a time when the only element in our favour was that of fire, the brazier a single beacon of compassion. I wonder to this day how we would have fared without it.

We huddled against the wind, a swirling canopy of snow above us, our bodies warmed on the one side, chilled on the other by the icy gusts. It was a situation, which compelled us continually to shift our positions as conditions demanded.

In my heart I felt it must have been nearing teatime, but — oh, God no! — it was as yet only dinnertime at the site. Four workmen including my father and the foreman squeezed past us and entered the hut, each one muttering uncomplimentary remarks about the weather. I knew then that my heart had misinformed me through sheer longing.

I watched the men as they dipped into their khaki haversacks from which each of them produced bread and cheese. I noted, too, that each of them prepared a mouthful in the same way. Dirt-grimed hands clutched both cheese and crusty bread while with heavy looking pocket knives they expertly cut portions of both and by pressing the two together between thumb and blade they lifted it to their mouths.

Watching them thus engaged I found myself wondering just for a moment why the workmen accepted my father in their midst, and yet were prepared to allow his family to remain outside. Perhaps men did not pass on infectious diseases, at least among themselves. I was far too miserable to enquire at the time, but upon reflection it remains an odd situation. My conclusion that day was simple: funny people grown-ups.

And so it was, with the four of us seated around that consolatory brazier, our clothing steaming all the time, the thick, wet flakes of snow continued to eddy ground-wards throughout that long afternoon. Most of it turned at once to icy, brown slush, but wherever the wind blew keenest it was preserved as white and desolate patches, which would stubbornly survive until that bitter blow either shifted or died away.

Our house was due to be opened at four-thirty, and right on the half hour we left the site and made our way towards Duck Lane. The man responsible was already at work and it did not take him long to break the seals. We then had to wait for the fumes to disperse.

We had eaten all of the sandwiches during the day and the basket, which lay at my feet, was quite empty. We had also long since consumed the contents of our thermos flask besides having emptied Father's flask, down at the swimming pool, and hunger and thirst allied themselves to the cold.

If ever a pathetic cluster of humanity stood in need of a Good Samaritan it was then. And one duly arrived.

We were sheltering from the snow and cowering from vicious blasts of icy wind in the stone-lined passage that cut through the row of hovels and led to the drying ground when Mrs. Phillips, a mother of three young children, appeared at the front entrance. She lived immediately next door to the passage and had obviously seen us arrive.

She was carrying a tray upon which were balanced four mugs of steaming soup and several slices of bread. Handing it to mother she said, "There you are, Vi. You'll all have pneumonia if they don't let you get indoors soon." She turned away and over her shoulder added, "Leave the tray at my doorstep when you've finished. It's cold enough to account for any germs, I should think."

It was a remarkable coincidence that soon after that dreadful day, at the Methodist Sunday School, we children were asked to single out in our hearts a special prayer for a special person. Need I say more?

CHAPTER
SIXTEEN

Farewell to the Beetles

Because of my ear trouble, besides losing a lot of schooling, I also lost a lot of working hours, but Miss Westcott was most considerate and kept my job open by paying her daily domestics a little extra for undertaking the duties that I normally performed. She was ever concerned about my welfare and always seemed very glad to welcome me back after a period of enforced absence. Only days after my bandages were permanently removed, I was back to work, which meant of course that I was also attending my own school once again.

Things in general were improving, if only slightly. The level of unemployment had dropped and Father was more at work than out of work. At Easter, which followed close upon that horrible day in the snow, Daisy left school. She went into daily domestic service and despite a small wage her contribution to the family income was most useful.

The row of seven hovels in Duck Lane remained under the sentence of condemnation and, under the auspices of a certain St Richard Society, we were among the first families destined to move to new accommodation in one of two blocks of flats: each containing four units, two up, two down.

These buildings were well on the way to completion and were situated at the far end of June Lane, not far from its junction with Petersfield Road. I got into the habit of running that way from school just to observe the progress, very often popping in to relay the latest information to Mother before going on to Lyndale School.

That summer, on the sixth of May, we celebrated the Silver Jubilee of the King's Accession. Poor Cecil missed all the fun, for he was still in hospital. We kept his commemorative mug for him, a dubious consolation I suspect.

It was an occasion that presented the town as a blaze of red, white and blue, but most of the festivities took place in the grounds of the Ruins and continued, I believe, a long time after dark. I missed out on its conclusion for by early evening I was completely fagged out.

A day crammed with excitement, it included many attractions such as fancy dress competitions, sporting events — one of which saw me as the winner of a long distance race — and all sorts of sideshows, the most popular being the coconut shy. There was a uniformed band that, it seemed to me, played non-stop all day, and there were mountains of free food including bars of Jubilee chocolate. This brought about the one and only disappointment of the day: it was the same as ordinary milk chocolate except for its wrapping of most colourful and patriotically designed emblems.

It was also a day that found me guilty of a memorable faux pas, although at the time of utterance it did not register with me. During the festival afternoon I saw Uncle Ern lurching along in the company of several men, all of who moved with a similar degree of unsteadiness. Having forsaken the beer tent they were heading for a patch of lush grass, which lay beneath a clump of elm tress. I watched with amusement as they each circled a small area — rather like some animals are wont to do — before selecting their places of repose. Finally they were all sprawled out beneath the shady boughs, where it seemed to me they all fell asleep immediately.

On that auspicious day Aunt Daisy had volunteered her services in the tea tent, and there she was working in the company of the mostly staid and pious wives and daughters of local dignitaries and professional people, when I burst upon the scene to report in a loud and excited voice that I was certain Uncle Ern was drunk.

I remember Mrs. Purser, the wife of my headmaster, looking at me disapprovingly from behind a big tea urn. Otherwise, among customers and staff alike, eyebrows were only momentarily raised in my direction and a discreet hush fell upon the proceedings. It was a response well intended, but I fear it succeeded only in aggravating my aunt's embarrassment. She made no answer. That she did not wish to receive such a communiqué in public, least of all in the sort of

178

company with whom she had been working, was made very clear to me on the following day.

Come midsummer Cecil was transferred from Brighton to the local cottage hospital where he spent several weeks in convalescence, coupled with the need to remain under close medical supervision, for he had of late been suffering from ear trouble.

Autumn saw our prospective home almost ready. We knew which flat — self-contained and upstairs — had been assigned to us, and Mother had already measured the windows for the purpose of making the curtains. The floor area, too, had been assessed in readiness for laying linoleum. Carpeting was a luxury we most certainly could not yet afford.

The family as a whole was completely thrilled. It was a marvellous prospect. The flat was comprised of three bedrooms, a kitchen, a front room, a bathroom and a lavatory. There was also a small larder and a fair amount of cupboard room. The front room and two of the bedrooms looked out over June Lane, each window providing a not too distant view of our school in Petersfield Road.

With the flat went a nice sized garden and a sturdily built shed. All around was greenery beneath a vast expanse of sky. What a contrast to our present situation!

If today I am considered a romantic with a leaning to all that is nostalgic, and I might well be, then I have remained unaltered for a very long time. Knowing then that I would soon be leaving Duck Lane, I began to try very hard to mentally record the little things that made up an average day's life for me in that environment: just so that in the future I could look back upon it and laugh, or cry. I wanted to take away with me a file of mental photographs, as it were, especially of the more endearing aspects, which before leaving I thought to be quite small in number. But I was to learn time has a habit of eroding the roughest edges of most recollections.

Over the years, that quite small number has increased considerably. From those early, squalid surroundings, there are projected upon my mind's eye scenes and objects of superb clarity. Such as my favourite red house brick, which in the winter was heated in the oven, then taken out to be wrapped in a piece of old blanket material before being carried off to bed, in lieu of the hot-water bottle we could not afford. As a small child, if perchance anyone else had taken my brick to bed, I would create such a commotion and demand that it be swapped for the alien one left for me. There were always three bricks in use, one for each of the three beds.

And how well I recall the single-handled, white-enamelled pot that stood, ever ready for nocturnal use, under the bed occupied by Cecil and me. Whenever one of us had need of its service, the person about to put it to use would first announce that a little chamber music was to be played, which would include a piece from Handel's Water Music. Neither of us knew anything about music. It was simply that reference to such things had been included in something I had read, and I had once used it as a joke when about to indulge in the said performance. At the time we thought it hilarious, and over the years it became a kind of humorous idiom, which was exclusive to us. We have often smiled about it in adult life.

Just as clearly remembered are the rows of wine-filled bottles, which stood nearby at the foot of the bed. Shoulder to shoulder they were mustered like immaculate ranks of guardsmen, their parade ground completely covering the well of the staircase. I have mentioned all this before, but now I see myself looking at the scene and wondering what was to happen to this vast array.

I supposed the cleaner-looking bottles, which stood together at one side, labelled and ready for consumption, would be consigned soon to the deeply recessed cupboards of our new home, and I presumed the ones still blowing their corks might perhaps be placed in the gloom of the shed, where they would go on popping and fizzing mostly unseen and unheard.

And would I ever sleep as soundly in a new room, even though in my old bed, without that soporific sibilance and that rooty, fruity aroma?

The smell of that wine and the sound of fermentation often reminded me of the occasion that found me indulging in what was considerably more than a finger-licking exercise. It was late in the morning, I was about six at the time, when with cup in hand I climbed the stairs and there, upon the landing, I decanted and drank a copious draught of parsnip wine. It was

181

probably fortunate for me that my maiden carousal was cut short by the intervention of Uncle Mossy who deprived me of both wine and vessels. Without a word to anyone, except for a few admonitory ones directed at me, he discreetly returned me to the little front room.

Later, Mother, who was unaware of all this, became very worried, not because I had fallen asleep immediately after my midday meal, but because I slept on throughout the afternoon and into the early evening. She and Father then decided to call in a doctor. It was at this point that Uncle Mossy was compelled to enlighten them as to the reason for my deep slumber. I awoke just in time to begin a good night's sleep.

But all that was in the past. Soon I would pay a last visit to the secret cache in the elderberry tree. There was no money there, only a small metal model of Sir Henry Seagrave's record-breaking car called, if I remember rightly, "Golden Arrow". Such data concerning the actual car was stamped upon the underside of the model. On the day I took my leave of Duck Lane I was to give this toy to my trusty friend, Dick. But I am hanged if I recall the reason for keeping the car in the tree.

The time was fast approaching when I would no longer scramble along the walls to Aunt Daisy's backyard. Neither would I see Nan and Uncle Mossy so often, and I would be leaving several good pals behind me.

During this period of waiting it seemed I talked to Nan quite a lot about poor Uncle Harry. Perhaps I felt

I was about to lose him, or his presence, for the second time. A long time after his death I had been taken to see his grave, where I understood more fully what death was all about, or, more correctly, how final it was. Until we moved from Duck Lane, I never felt that Uncle Harry was far away.

At Carshalton I had not enjoyed myself half as much during that summer as I had on previous occasions. I had been far too eager to get back to Midhurst lest the family moved in my absence. I so much wanted to be in on the act. Nothing else had really mattered during those final weeks except that they might disappear quickly before the oncoming autumn, a season for us so full of promise.

Autumn was with us and still we waited. The flat had been made ready, but a lot of time was given in those days for a newly built place to properly dry out. Then, at long last, a date was set; there was just one week to go.

For me it also meant there were but seven days remaining during which I could attempt to achieve a burning ambition. Before leaving Duck Lane I must conquer the "stink-pipe": more properly defined as an iron sewer vent — about a foot in diameter and some twenty feet tall, surmounted by what looked very much like a spiked coronet. It stood at the northern end of the lane, and boys of all ages — probably since it was first erected — had made countless attempts to climb to the top.

It was mainly the early teenagers and upwards who succeeded, and a lot of that success depended upon the prevailing weather. If it were damp it was most difficult to obtain a firm grip with hands, knees or feet, all of which were needed in an ascent that invariably resulted in a slippery descent long before any real elevation had been reached.

Under good conditions, with boys of my age, it was quite an achievement to reach the halfway mark. At the age of eleven and only two days before leaving for June Lane, after umpteen attempts, I made it. My head rose above the coronet and feeling quite sick with fright, as I looked down from my precarious perch, I was nevertheless triumphant. I scented success. Phew, what a smell! It was no small wonder that grown-ups were always reprimanding kids who were caught climbing that unhealthy object. It was the very last of my athletic undertakings in Duck Lane.

It was the end of a chapter, not of the book. Why then, these tiny ripples of regret?

Another day had passed, and the next would find me paying my last farewells to the black beetles and fleas, although I was not sure what form this would take. The coal cupboard was empty, for Father had bagged up all the fuel ready for transportation. I dare not investigate the cupboard in his presence, but I imagined just how easy it would be to club a few beetles to death. They were, for the first time, without the coal under which they had always sought refuge, disappearing into the heap, their jet black bodies perfectly camouflaged. Since the fumigation, they and the fleas seemed to have grown both in strength and number. Due, I suppose, to the survival of the fittest.

One more night under the skilling and in the morning one last visit to the communal lavatories. The tin bath, which hung outside upon the back wall would be taken with us, but would never be required again for bathing. The oil lamp and the candles, too, would go with us, but only to be held in reserve in case of an electrical fault.

We were about to move into a realm of sheer luxury or so it seemed to us. Yet, in the flood of happiness that welled within me, I acknowledge there were little drops of sadness.

As we talked in bed that night, Cecil, newly arrived from that long spell in hospital, told me that he, too, felt a wee bit sad. But, came the morning, and excitement alone prevailed.

It was a Saturday, and Uncle Ern had borrowed or hired the big lorry, which he drove for the mill. It was easily roomy enough to convey all our meagre possessions in one journey. Every member of the family assisted, including Marjorie in her small way. It would be more accurate to say that all our furniture was soon aboard the lorry, rather than to say the lorry was loaded. We were ready to be on our way.

All of our old neighbours, or so it seemed to me, had turned out in the lane to bid and wave us farewell. One lasting memory of that confused and emotional moment was the realisation that tears were falling from the eyes of my old pal, Dick. I am certain I had never before seen him cry. He was just not that type.

★ ★ ★

Waving and calling our goodbyes we moved off, heading for June Lane via West Street and Petersfield Road: a more easily negotiated route with such a large vehicle.

That particular morning I had to desert the lorry long before it reached its destination. I merely hung on to Uncle Ern's cab door until he was about to turn into West Street. Here I jumped off, leaving the rest of my family aboard, some up front, some in the back. I had to go to work. Lyndale School awaited.

I did my usual Saturday morning stint of about two hours, mostly cleaning shoes and cutlery, although I do remember sweeping up leaves in the courtyard and wondering all the time how things were progressing at our new home. I did not ask or look for extra work that morning, entering my hours upon the calendar just as soon as I was able, and slipping off at the earliest convenient moment.

Eagerly I trotted up June Lane. It was nearly dinnertime, but the thought of food had not entered my mind. When I arrived things were amazingly shipshape. The floor covering and the curtains had been put in place some days before; nevertheless, I thought everyone concerned had done jolly well.

A delightful first impression of our new home remains so very clear in my mind. It is of walking with stockinged feet into the front room to be greeted with the sight of the old articles of furniture arrayed in their modern surroundings, and feeling beneath my feet the incredibly level and slippery linoleum: a far cry from the rough, brick floor of the Duck Lane hovel, where the jagged and undulating surface caused the linoleum to crack all over the place, no matter what precautions were taken. I had left my shoes at the foot of the stairs.

Mother swiftly prepared our first meal, sausage and mash, at St Richard Flats and a six-course meal at the Savoy could not have been devoured more happily. We sat at the table in the kitchen, from the windows of which we could view countless acres of meadow and woodland.

It was not just a new home. Already it was a completely new life.

CHAPTER
SEVENTEEN

Mixed Fortunes

The swimming pool had been completed, but Father remained in employment at a building site somewhere in Easebourne. Daisy, at about this time, changed her job. She moved on to Lyndale School, where, just before Christmas, my hours were cut down. I no longer worked late afternoons, only Saturday mornings, for the numbers of pupils at Lyndale had steadily declined, and the daily staff were able to cope with the shoe-cleaning task.

As always, we thoroughly enjoyed Christmas, even more so I would say, for here everything was so much cosier and cleaner. But some things remained the same. The old gramophone opened up on the happy morning with "Hark the Herald Angels Sing", just as it had done, year after year, at Duck Lane.

The Christmas tree had been brought from the allotment, for Father had not yet relinquished the plot of land, which lay just about halfway between our new home and our old. But the tree, having served its festive duty, was transplanted into our new garden where it continued to flourish for many more years.

★   ★   ★

The new year arrived, and another term had started at school. Marjorie, too, had begun her schooldays. She was in Miss Attree's infant class.

Since I was no longer gainfully employed after school hours I was sometimes called upon to cart coke for our own use, in the same old truck. There was little hope of expanding business at this end of June Lane. There were not enough prospective customers, there being only eight flats and some half a dozen homesteads in the entire local vicinity. I was not too unhappy about it; it was an awfully long haul from the gasworks to our place. Most of the families around us had their own trucks, anyway — and the means of propulsion.

I was back to square one really for, apart from my Saturday morning's earnings at Lyndale, my annual income was again dependent upon the proceeds from Goodwood Week, and the acorn harvest, which followed close upon it.

But at least I was most admirably situated for both events.

There were, literally, hundreds of oak trees all around us. One massive and prolific tree stood very near to our front door and yearly deposited at least a quarter of its yield upon our garden. Even little Marjorie lent a hand at gathering this. I do not recall that either Cecil or I gave her very much for her pains, but what could one so young possibly want with money? A fair and unanswerable question we thought at the time.

With regard to Goodwood Week, we occupied a marvellous new position, easily the best in the district.

Immediately opposite the sandy playground at our school, and just around the corner from our flat, there stood a public house called the Half Moon. It was sited hard against a rough, gravel-surfaced drive, which looped in from the junction of June Lane with Petersfield Road and rejoined the main road very nearly opposite the infants playground at the other end of the school.

The drive dipped below the level of the main road and the two were separated by a sloping grass bank, some six yards across at the halfway mark, and roughly crescent-shaped. The primary function of this drive was to provide access not only to the Half Moon, but also to four cottages, which stood adjacent to the inn, ranging to a point opposite the school buildings.

It served a dual purpose. This gravelled service lane provided a lengthy pull-in, open at both ends to the main road. The Half Moon was a small, usually quiet pub, but I once saw eleven coaches (by then we no longer called them charabancs) lined along that drive at one time, all en route home from Goodwood.

On the lawn at the back of the inn, a marquee was erected every year, wherein refreshments of a less stimulating nature might be obtained, mainly tea and sandwiches. This part of the business created temporary employment for quite a number of local women, my mother included, and was a pleasant diversion from their otherwise humdrum lives.

But, so far as we kids were concerned, it was at the front of the pub where the fun was to be found. Not so much in the morning, although there were always a few coppers to be cadged or scrambled for. It was in the evening that the real fun started.

The somewhat undignified scrambling for rusty coppers was cut down by the introduction of competitions arranged for us by various members of coach parties. Simple running races, up and down the drive, alongside the row of coaches, were swiftly organised with handicaps applied according to sex and age.

I recall one occasion when a very popular man we knew by the nickname "Sticky" — he came on all four days every year — arranged a long-jump competition on a triangular piece of grassland, which lay close by the pub. I won that, and I clearly remember the prize-money amounted to one whole shilling (5p).

I did fairly well in the running events, although it was always in the longer races that I shone.

There were from time to time, mostly in the late afternoon, spiteful confrontations with small gangs of kids moving up from the town. Realising the Half Moon had become the most lucrative pitch in the district they attempted to encroach upon what we considered to be our territory. We easily drove them off, simply because we outnumbered them. It was no good for them to come in overwhelming hordes, for this they were aware would defeat the whole object. There was obviously a limit to the amount of money the race-goers could or would distribute; acknowledged, therefore, was the fundamental fact too many kids made for too little shares.

★　★　★

Standing in the open doorway of the public bar one evening my interest was instantly aroused when I saw a sixpenny piece rolling straight towards me from the confines of the crowded room. Fool that I was, I hesitated a fraction of a second too long and watched it disappear, almost at my feet, down an iron grating. Despite the fading light, I saw the coin lying on a carpet of dirt about two feet below ground level.

Sixpence had considerable purchasing power in those days: it would buy three packets of potato crisps. The press of people around me made it impossible to do anything about it at the time, but I resolved to retrieve that sixpence somehow.

The grating was cemented at the edges and I could see there was no way I could lift it. This called for a more subtle approach.

I began to ponder.

Early next morning I left home and ambled down June Lane towards the pub, carrying an old walking stick. It was only a couple of hundred yards or so and I was in no hurry, for I was steadily champing upon a piece of chewing gum in preparation for the execution of my overnight plan.

I reached the pub and all was quiet. Then a man came riding slowly along the main road on a squeaky bicycle, and I waited for him to pass by. I was not in the process of committing a crime; I simply wanted that sixpence for myself, with no half shares given for any help I might receive.

First I stuck the piece of chewing gum to the tip of the walking stick. Very carefully I guided the stick between the bars of the grating. There was just width enough. One quick press and the sixpence adhered to the gum. After which, all that was required was a steady withdrawal and with bated breath this was achieved.

It was a splendid start to the day. I had earned a tanner before breakfast. I washed the piece of chewing gum under the kitchen tap, for as yet it had not lost its minty flavour, and I chewed upon it until breakfast. Father had left for work even before I had risen that morning, but I was able to boast to Mother of my achievement. She was highly amused.

My latter references to the local activities during Goodwood Week, and to the gathering of acorns in such close proximity to home, are included in my tale in order to project a general description of our vastly improved surroundings. But such considerations slightly overrun my story.

Soon after our first Christmas at the flat, Cecil began to suffer terribly from both ears, and subsequently entered the cottage hospital where he underwent an operation for double mastoiditis. His life, like mine, might well have been spared through surgery, but again like me he was plagued with ear trouble which continued into adult life.

Daisy, at the same time, fell sick with rheumatic fever, and she was whisked off to a hospital at Chichester. Although initially she was very ill, she did make a complete recovery with none of the recurring symptoms associated with that disease in those days.

Our change of environment had so far no effect regarding the state of family health, but no doubt these recent illnesses were but legacies of Duck Lane. We could only hope for better days.

Cecil returned home a long time before Daisy was discharged and he was soon attending school again, although with ears well protected against the late winter winds.

Now that Marjorie, too, was attending school, Mother was in a position to take on a part-time job. This was directly opposed to the more noble of Father's instincts. The idea of wives going out to work was not easily accepted by some of the more old-fashioned members of the community, including Father, despite the fact that he earned barely enough to support us. Fifty years on it is laughable, the winds of change have certainly seen to that, but at that time it was, I suppose, a matter of pride.

Mother was more practical and Father's objection was overruled. She became charlady at the Midhurst Catholic Church, which was structurally attached to — of all places — my one time favourite haunt, the Wheatsheaf. It was here, working in the house of the Great Architect Himself, as it were, that Mother very nearly had an early confrontation with Him.

When kneeling in the aisle, not in prayerful worship, but while engaged in scrubbing the floor, Mother had from time to time experienced a peculiar tingling sensation, sometimes in her arms, sometimes in her legs. At first she thought perhaps she might be trapping a nerve in her back simply by the process of kneeling and, since it did not incapacitate her in any way, she carried on and ignored it as best she could.

The floor was scrubbed once a week so that it was months before it dawned upon her that this strange tingling sensation seemed to intensify in one particular part of the aisle. Even then, because it was at the end of the aisle where she completed her scrubbing, she was inclined to attribute the increase in sensation to the amount of time she had remained in a kneeling posture.

But one day, having slopped a little more water than usual in that area, she received, not a tingle, but a distinct jolt. Mother realised that not even a badly trapped nerve would engender such a thumping reaction as that. The trouble was not within her; it came from a source somewhere without.

On her way home she called in at the priest's house and duly reported her experience. Immediately, investigations were made and a badly damaged electric cable was discovered under the floor, damaged, it was supposed, when the floor was recently renovated. An electrician considered Mother to be the luckiest person alive.

Mother remarked jokingly that she would probably not require the use of curling-tongs on her hair for a long time to come.

CHAPTER
EIGHTEEN

Fisticuffs

It was towards the end of our first winter at June Lane that I finally reaped the benefit of those early boxing lessons. Father had kept me up to scratch in all the skills that Uncle Harry had taught me. In fact we still possessed the boxing gloves, but even my small pair were then dangerously tattered.

Bill, my companion of the icehouse episode, was to bring this about. He was not in my estimation a bully, but he loved to fight and he was pretty tough. I have since felt that he needed to prove himself against me and his approach to this end was through Cecil.

At school, during morning playtime, Bill, for no apparent reason, continually harassed my brother by pushing him around, tripping him up and threatening, above all, to smack his ears. I am certain he would never have done this, but, quite naturally, it frightened poor Cecil.

Bill was, in our schoolboy vernacular, "a rough handful". Nervously I challenged him. He picked up the metaphorical gauntlet with alacrity. We squared up and exactly at that moment a bell rang out, but it was the bell that heralded the end of playtime. We vehemently agreed to postpone the fight until dinnertime.

The teachers usually remained inside the school during the midday break, except for Miss Parker who cycled home for her meal and Mr Purser who walked home for his. We waited until they and most of the pupils had disappeared and then the battle commenced. There was a grown-up audience, for working nearby on the main road was a gang of some half a dozen council workers. They straightened up to watch.

Boys of our age, we were only eleven, do not generally fight with clenched fists, at least not for long. Most schoolboy scraps were decided by a mauling, wrestling bout, which usually finished with both antagonists on the ground, the one ending up on top proclaiming himself the winner. This was a fight with a difference.

Bill knew all about my early boxing lessons; he was going to use his fists all the way, too. And this he did. Not expertly, fortunately for me, but he swung long looping punches that, had I not maintained a good defence, would most surely have punctured my eardrums.

The weather was cold and I was wearing a pair of old gloves, which had been discarded by my mother. The number of times that left glove hit Bill smack on the nose would have so pleased Uncle Harry.

I scarcely used my right at all, except for picking off his violent left swings. The power behind his punches caused me to retreat in the opening stages, but I was unhurt behind a solid guard, and I knew that if I remained cool and kept pumping away with that straight left, I would ride out the storm and go on to win.

Bill was throwing fewer punches by then, and they were nothing like so heavy. With a badly cut bottom lip and blood spurting from his nose his face looked a bit like a map of the British Empire, red all over the place. But he was tough and a terrier at heart, and so the battle raged on. The day was mine and I knew it, but my left glove was soaked with blood before Bill would admit defeat.

It had not been entirely due to my skill and certainly not to my strength that a fast congealing crimson mask spread fairly evenly over Bill's features. He had bored in recklessly, leaving his face completely unprotected from beginning to end. I felt both elated and worried at the same time. It was nice to have won so handsomely, but I hoped Bill was not hurt too badly. As for myself, I had come out of it unscathed, except for the bruises that I knew would soon appear upon my arms and shoulders.

Bill turned away and made for home. The council workers cheered me, just the way the Sunday morning audience had done years ago when I regularly defeated Uncle Harry. One of them came over and asked to know who had taught me to box like that. I told him all about Uncle Harry. The man nodded knowingly, "That explains it, I knowed 'im well."

With the noisy compliments of the workmen still falling upon my none too keen ears I crossed the main road and went off round the corner to June Lane. I joined Cecil and Marjorie in the kitchen of the flat where they were just about finishing their share of the sandwiches, which Mother always prepared and left for us on the days she went out to work.

I explained my reason for being late home and, for some quite illogical reason, made them promise not to tell our parents. I demanded absolute secrecy, for I had a strange feeling of guilt about it all. An ordinary scrap was one thing, but the mess I had made of Bill's face still worried me. It was not out of compassion; I was beginning to wonder what his parents would say or do about it.

During the main meal early that evening, Mother remarked that she had seen young Bill soon after midday in Midhurst with his face all blooded, and sporting a split and swollen lip. Marjorie solemnly looked down at her plate. Cecil gave out a little chuckle, and Father eyed him suspiciously. Mother had observed my blush. I felt at that moment that if she did not already know the truth, it was a certainty she soon would.

I produced her old, bloodstained, left glove from my jacket pocket and related the whole story. Father was unreservedly delighted; I do not think he was ever more proud of me. Mother was not entirely displeased, albeit she was a trifle concerned about the likelihood of repercussions.

As it turned out, she need not have worried. There was none, except for a mild and cursory reprimand addressed to both ex-combatants by Mr. Purser.

The affair was brought to the headmaster's attention on the following day only by the badly swollen lip Bill had sustained, and which by then was the one remaining sign of our bloody encounter. Bill insisted it was the result of a fall, purely accidental, but school-age tongues wag loosely and the truth came out.

Before we were dismissed Mr. Purser commented upon Bill's mendacity. "Bill," he said, in no way speaking sharply, "By endeavouring to shield Ron, you lied to me, and I cannot truly condone this. I will, nevertheless, overlook your conduct on this occasion, for I find your motive quite laudable. Now lads, away with you and no more fighting."

Bill went on in his rough and ready way throughout the remainder of his school days, but never again did he cross swords with me. I was not too sorry about that, for I was fully aware that one of his haymakers, landing on target, would very nearly decapitate me.

It is sad to reflect that, as a direct result of Adolf Hitler's recent dramatic rise to total power in far away Germany, Bill was already halfway through his life.

CHAPTER
NINETEEN

Starling Pie and Other Sports

If there be a hereafter, and if, in accordance with the words of better informed men than I, our ultimate destination is dependent upon the outcome of a celestial inquisition, I fear that one of the chief prosecutors engaged upon my case will be one St Francis of Assisi.

If the accusations are delivered in chronological order, then the trial will almost certainly begin with an account of my beetle-bashing activities at Duck Lane. I have already decided to plead for extenuation by virtue of my extreme youth at the time. On those same grounds, I doubt that they would throw the puppy-washing episode at me at all. In the case of the beetles, I would go on to say that by my actions I saved an untold number of them from a far worse end: that of being shovelled up with the coal, all alive and well, only to be cremated.

St Francis will know that in later years I was responsible for the death of many a succulent rabbit, a few wild pigeons and the odd pheasant or two. There were also many fishes whose lives were curtailed by my riverside operations, but curiously enough, as far as I recall, only one wild duck.

These transgressions, I hope, will be weighed against the systematic duplicity, which daily provided the abattoirs of the world with semi-domesticated creatures who suddenly come face to face with the ghastly truth that their trust in mankind was sadly misplaced. At least my victims never once trusted me.

I, as a country boy, had been brought up to fish, hunt and kill, but never wantonly, especially on the last count. My prosecutor will perhaps cede a point or two on that score, but the very moment he refers to a certain starling pie I shall stand shamefaced, for even in this world the memory of that pie or rather more its contents still troubles me.

Cecil was my accomplice or, more accurately, I was his accomplice, for it was he who brought home the whole idea. Someone had told him that starlings were an absolute delicacy when baked in a pie. He imparted this information late one afternoon and we decided there and then to have such a meal for tea.

Armed with two catapults and an old air rifle, and with a pocket full of breadcrumbs to be used as bait, we set out to lure and to kill our feathered prey. Treachery coupled with good marksmanship soon paid off. We returned bearing the bodies of seven fair-sized starlings. It was fortunate they were prime specimen, for there is not much to a starling once it is plucked and prepared. Indeed the seven combined looked a pretty small offering to large and interested appetites.

We next attempted to make a pie and failed abysmally. It was at this stage that Mother arrived home and, after much persuasion, grudgingly agreed to make one for us. She was not at all happy about it, but she had to admit the starlings had indisputably reached a point of no return. She sternly told us she was about to cook her first starling pie and that it would most certainly be the last.

Father came in just as we were finishing the meal. He disapproved of the whole project and he said so without fear of argument. Out of interest, he did accept a piece of a tiny breast, all that was left on the pie dish. He chewed at the meat rather nosily, smacking his lips and sucking hard at it in an effort to derive the maximum flavour from such a minute portion.

"Not bad," he said, as he swallowed the last fleshy fragment of our catch, "but bear this in mind. I'd sooner hear a bird sing than sizzle."

My brother and I, alert to the underlying menace in his voice, quickly agreed in front of him that we found the flesh of a starling far too bitter for us and we would never want to try it again. But secretly I was of the opinion that it would become a popular dish if a starling took on the proportions of a pheasant.

Nevertheless, just as soon as the excitement and novelty of it all was consigned to history, I felt extremely penitent about the whole business.

There is nothing brave or commendable in killing wild birds. We had not been motivated by hunger. It had been a wanton act produced by an abundance of cruelty. This I freely admitted and I knew full well that, even in those hard days spent at Duck Lane, Father would have bridled at the thought of supplying the principal ingredient for a starling pie.

All of these angles were discussed with Cecil, but he was unrepentant and even argumentative. "Dad eats all sorts of meat. Why not a wild bird? What's the difference?"

I never did think of an adequate reply, so if it comes to the pinch I might catch out St. Francis by employing the same argument. In any event I should get off, for my learned friend will know of my contrition. "He that repenteth . . ."

At about this time, a slight but perceptible advance in the general standard of living was evolving. Why, even I noted that very young children played with real marbles, never having to make do with rolled up woodlice, as was the case in my early experience.

Wallowing in this new-found opulence, we bought our first wireless set on hire-purchase. It was a Cosser Jubilee Model and it cost all of six pounds, which, paid off at the weekly rate of half-a-crown (12½p), took just one year to clear.

I knew more about wireless programmes than anyone at home, so in the early stages I was chief selector. This was because Uncle Ern had possessed a radio for some years and, although it oscillated rather loudly at times, I had become a frequent listener. I was familiar with most of the sponsored programmes on Radio Luxembourg and I knew many of the songs, like the one as sung by the Ovaltinies little girls and boys, all the way through.

But it was to be on our own set, not long after its installation, that I would learn that a wireless could provide a far more useful service than simply picking up music and plays, and the commentaries of football matches with the square one, square two and so on method of describing where the ball was currently being played on the pitch.

I, and millions more on that chill January day, heard over the air the sad news that King George V had passed away. It was the very first really grave announcement that I ever heard on the wireless.

Strangely enough Father, who had been the least enthusiastic over the contemplated purchasing of a radio, was fast becoming the number one fan in our family, although never to the detriment of his beloved garden. The wireless was primarily a winter evening pastime, but we no longer played cards or dominoes, or any other such games on the scale that we used to, not even on a wet evening in summer. Times were already a'changing.

In addition to the garden, which we inherited with the tenancy of the flat, we were given an extension at the far end of the existing plot of at least as much ground as was already under cultivation without having to pay extra rent. Father was delighted and we subsequently bade farewell to the June Lane allotment. All crops would be close at hand.

With regard to his employment, yet another development was working in Father's favour. A one-time boggy meadow lay between our block of flats and the school football ground. This was being drained even as we had moved to June Lane. It was bristling with short wooden pegs, marking out the footings for buildings soon to be erected, six pairs of council houses to be precise. Father sought and found employment at this site, literally right at his doorstep.

Things were looking up, but there were still numerous economies to be observed. A gas geyser provided us with hot water, but it cost at least sixpence to produce enough warm water for even a shallow bath. In the interests of necessary frugality, Cecil and I, for example, would share a drawn bath, one following the other in rapid succession, the order of entry being decided, on most occasions, by the toss of a coin.

Should any one of us kids remain in the lavatory for more than a couple of minutes with the light on Mother or Father would call out a sentence, which usually ran thus: "Put out that light if you're going to sleep in there."

Also, in the early days at our new home we were not permitted to read in bed. All reading had to be done before retiring, lest too big a strain be placed upon meter requirements. Exceptions were made in cases of illness.

But all of this we cheerfully accepted. Life was infinitely better than at any time in Duck Lane. Gradually, because of Father's regular employment, Mother's part-time job, and Daisy's small contribution — she had returned to work in the late spring — the economic conditions under which we lived took a firm step in the right direction. The lowest level of a modest existence had been reached.

We had butter on our bread on Sundays, and occasionally herrings for tea on a Saturday. These sorts of things cost the budget a little extra and were by the way of small treats. But, in the main, we ate very well because of the ever present garden produce. It would have been possible to have obtained meat in plenty without the need to pay for it at all. The river ran close by and in the surrounding fields were rabbits galore. Naturally, we did avail ourselves of these succulent resources from time to time, but it was as an addition to an already improving diet.

In March, despite my hitherto erratic attendance at school, my ears were still a source of intermittent trouble; I was considered a good enough scholar by Mr. Purser to sit for an entry examination to the local Grammar School.

That I failed at the age of eleven and again at the age of twelve has never ceased to intrigue me.

Without I trust appearing immodest, I can only state in all honesty that lesser scholars than I passed or were passed, and all examinees know in their heart of hearts whether or not they have done well enough. I felt on both occasions that I had, with a little to spare, too.

I make no excuses, no accusations, but I wonder to this day why the preliminary paper, apart from requesting my name and address, was headed by the demand to know my father's occupation. I faithfully wrote "Labourer" against the question, although what this information had to do with my scholastic career I knew not.

After my second failure Mr. Purser seemed more embarrassed than anyone, a reaction that culminated in his sending a note to my parents in which it was suggested that both failures were directly attributable to my persistent ear trouble, and that he could offer no other explanation for such an academic upset. Well, that was his opinion in writing and in his position diplomacy was of paramount importance. He committed himself no further.

Overall, there would seem to be one redeeming feature. At least, because of my disappointing failure my parents were spared the crippling expense of providing a school uniform and other accessories. Or even worse the embarrassment of not being able to. I remember them mentioning the sum of eight pounds.

To Father that amount of money represented something in excess of four weeks' full wages. I employ the word "full" for, if at any time it rained hard enough to prevent work from being carried out, it simply meant a loss of wages for the duration of the inclement weather. On the building sites they called it "wet time". There was no such thing as a guaranteed minimum wage.

In winter, freezing conditions were often more of a threat to the financial stability of a building worker than to his immediate physical well-being. Such conditions persisting could only result in a long layoff at a building site, bringing about the inevitable and familiar monetary crisis.

Before buying an item under a hire purchase agreement, for example our newly acquired radio, it was prudent to first assess the extent of sympathetic understanding that might be expected from the retailer concerned. In the event of such a financial calamity it was to be hoped that he would exercise patience and wait until the crisis was over before demanding further instalments and, above all, that he would not resort to applying for a repossession order.

Perhaps, in the field of education, the powers-that-be had taken into account all such contingencies when they drew up the paper subtitled "Father's Occupation".

Father, bless him, gave little thought to artistic and academic accomplishment. He had no real propensity towards education at all. His chief aspiration in life was to be recognised as a good general worker. "I might not be much at words or figures," he would say, "but I know 'ow to use a pick and shovel."

His advice to both Cecil and me was always along these lines. "Never mind yer books and things. Get yerself a reputation as a good grafter, and if there's any work about, you'll stand a chance."

Just down the lane, in the grounds at the back of the Half Moon, a small workshop occupying part of what had once been a large stable was used by a bespectacled, middle-aged man, who modestly called himself a sign writer. This workshop was more like an artist's studio, with several paintings adorning the walls. Scattered about on a long, wide workbench were mahlsticks and palettes lying around amongst tins of all sorts of paint.

In fact, he had in his younger days been a scenic painter for a number of London theatres, besides gilding and painting many a vast and decorative auditorium. He was greatly gifted and highly skilled in all aspects of his trade, and for a hobby he painted both landscapes and portraits.

We became firm friends and I would stand and watch him for hours as he exercised his talents so effortlessly. Matching marble with paint, applying gold leaf to glass, none of it was work to him. It was a beloved art and it provided a living.

I have envied Joe Ward, for so was his name, ceaselessly from those days on. "Ronnie," he used to say quite frequently, "only fools and donkeys work."

Remembering my father's advice, to an eleven years' old boy, these two conflicting philosophies presented a bit of a puzzle. But at that age I did not dwell upon it.

In the late summer of that year I took my annual holiday at Carshalton, but I did not return to my Saturday morning job at Lyndale School. Miss Westcott had been forced to economise even further and had recently been keeping me on only out of kindness.

Just before I had left for my holiday I did, however, manage to pass on a fair amount of fruit to the kids of Duck Lane, employing my original method and the simple signalling arrangements in unison with my old pal, Dick, who still lived next door to my grandmother.

Looking back over the years, I still feel a bit of a scoundrel about it all, but the children of Duck Lane had been grateful, and the crime remained undetected — an almost incredible fact.

In all other respects it would seem that I had done my duty towards Miss Westcott in an exemplary manner for, when she finally closed the school and retired to a small cottage not far away, she would often prevail upon me to help her out whenever her little garden grew out of hand. The wage remained the same: sixpence per hour.

Daisy, too, had by this time left Lyndale School, and was a daily domestic servant to an extremely nice family. She was so much better in both health and spirit.

In consequence of my association with Joe Ward, who paid a nominal rent for his workshop to the landlady of the Half Moon, I began to do little jobs for her in and around the pub. Mrs. Goatcher by name, she was a widow and she ran the business with the help of her niece, called Louie. I was never regularly employed by Mrs. Goatcher, who, incidentally, was an elderly, very Victorian-looking lady, who appeared to me at the time to be an older version of Miss Westcott. I simply did odd jobs for her whenever required, even after I left school.

I completely forget what she paid me for these intermittent tasks, which covered a wide selection ranging from weeding the borders of the lawn to cleaning out the drains around the pub, but one remuneration always was a glass of that delicious yellow lemonade, which never failed to remind me of those far off Sundays at the Wheatsheaf with Uncle Harry.

Although in so many ways our move to June Lane had created a new kind of life, a lot of our outdoor activities remained the same. We continued to fish for eels, accepting the occasional errant trout should it be disposed to take the bait, but we patrolled a different stretch of water, for we fished to the west of Midhurst.

I must observe that, so far as Father and I were concerned, fishing had become more of a hobby. There was no longer the urgency to catch fish for food. But Cecil had begun to take a tremendous interest in fishing. Indeed, he was already displaying a fundamental curiosity in just about every aspect of country life, far more than I had at his age. Gradually Father and I left it all to him, for he was able to provide us with our requirements quite easily, and we turned our backs upon what had once been a principal pastime. Cecil took over the sack of equipment and for the most part patrolled the riverbank alone.

I certainly did not desert the river, for it was along that same stretch of water that I learnt to swim.

My outdoor energies were directed more towards the football field in winter and swimming in the summer, a risky sport to engage in when one considers the state of my ears. And yet I became a very good underwater swimmer. As for professional medical opinions, one doctor would say nay and another yea. I think it depended upon the condition of my ears at the time of examination. I did continue to suffer bouts of ear trouble, but it was — as it had always been — mainly during the winter months. In the summer I carried on swimming.

Forsaking the quieter stretches of river near home, I very often met up with a school pal of mine, Charles Lusty, with the purpose of swimming together at a very popular bathing spot near the Ruins: part of the length of river so familiar to me in my Duck Lane days. Even on the coolest of summer days there seemed to be a number of local Spartans in that vicinity ready to defy an onslaught of gooseflesh.

Now Charles's father was adamant that the first most important lesson in life was that of learning to swim without which ability, should certain unfortunate circumstances arise of an aquatic nature, all other tuition was rendered, in a matter of moments, worthless.

Such was the philosophy of Mr. Lusty, middle-aged, tall and slim, and still a good athlete, despite increasingly frequent attacks of asthma. And he did something about it.

There were no facilities in the district where the pupils of our school or of the little village schools might learn to swim. The river was the only solution. Better to make a playmate of it than to accept it as a potential, silent killer. There were those who disagreed, regarding pollution as its real danger. Be that as may be, I am convinced that the river claimed more victims through drowning than by any other means. And yet the great majority of school-leavers throughout the period in question were unable to swim.

Employed to tend the sick at the local workhouse, Mr. Lusty was not a well-off man, but he was a qualified nurse with a nature that could not be more suited to his profession. With a family of three children, how he was able to produce all those moth-eaten, tatty old shorts and costumes for the use of so many would-be swimmers is beyond me. Perhaps he had been a beachcomber at some time.

There were quite a few lads at that time who had never worn underpants. Some had never heard of them. Therefore it was unlikely that these lads would possess a luxury item such as bathing trunks. Mr. Lusty provided.

Before entering the water to instruct his pupils, he would sit upon the grass, high on the riverbank, doling out all manner of costumes to those in need, and there were plenty in that category, asking at the same time for confirmation of their parents' approval. Some even produced written evidence.

And then it was everybody into the water. There were, of course, a few older pupils who had attained a fair degree of ability and for them Mr. Lusty, a very good swimmer himself, would demonstrate many advanced strokes and, more importantly, the various techniques used in lifesaving. But most of the time his heart and eyes were set firmly upon the beginners, all of whom initially stayed close to the bank in the shallows.

When the time came to pack it up for the day he would gather in the costumes and carry them home as one big bundle. Mrs. Lusty then rinsed them out and hung them on the washing-line in readiness for the next occasion.

I am certain, because of his innate modesty, Mr. Lusty did not realise how much his pupils thought of him. Long after he had left for home it was usual for the lads to sit in little groups along the river bank, falling out over many things, as boys are wont to do, but always in full agreement as to what a great guy Mr. Lusty was. To which I add in conclusion that men such as he are few and far between.

Despite the shortening dole queues, the amusing term "enough for a latch-lifter" was still in common use. It was an expression hanging over from the days of rife unemployment and meant quite simply that if a man had as much as twopence in his pocket, the price of half a pint of mild beer, he was able to lift the latch of a public house door and enter with head held high, even though the length of his stay would certainly depend upon the amount of charity to be found within. I know that in the bad old days my father, along with Uncle Harry, had many times been fortunate in gaining an evening of lubricated pleasure by putting over their extensive repertoire of mostly comic songs to an appreciative audience made up of better-off members of the community. And all because they had possessed "enough for a latch-lifter".

The expression had more recently taken on a wider meaning. It was used as a substitute for the term "beer money", indicating there was extra cash to be had by indulging in a sideline of some sort. A furry beast of bank and hedgerow was about to provide Father many times from then on with "enough for a latch-lifter". Rabbit hunting or more hopefully, rabbit catching, was a new activity afforded to us by our immediate surroundings. This profitable recreation was more of a grown-up's pastime, but we kids were often permitted to go along. Good behaviour and the ability to make ourselves useful when the occasion arose was all that was required of us.

A rabbit, besides providing the basis of a succulent meal, was endowed with a useful and widely used pelt, which when treated with alum could be preserved until enough were collected to make a sale worthwhile. The healthy rabbits of those days presented a very saleable commodity, especially at almost giveaway prices.

My father's sudden adherence to this latest sport was brought about by a friendship struck up with a Mr. Phillips, better known to all close associates as Pop. Pop lived in one of a pair of farm cottages, just across the lane, almost opposite our block of flats. He had recently lost his wife to a long and cruel illness. Because they had not long moved to this district, their son, Harry, continued to attend his old school by cycling a round trip of about four miles each day. He was ten months my senior, his father eight years older than mine. Both became an integral part of my life.

216

Pop possessed all the necessary equipment required for proficient rabbit catching: plenty of nets, a twelve-bore shotgun and, the most important thing by far, two cages full of ferrets.

Always working on the farmland, which virtually surrounded us, Pop was pretty conversant with the dispositions of the local rabbit colonies. He made astute observations during his daily toil, and at any suitable time — mainly at weekends — he and my father would set out to exploit this knowledge. Harry and I and, very often, young Cecil would trail along with them.

Upon reaching a selected rabbit warren we carefully placed the nets over all the holes. If we did happen to miss one, and this was easily possible in thick undergrowth, the gun might prove a useful backup. A ferret was hauled from the sack, in which two or three of them were unceremoniously carried together with all the necessary paraphernalia, and Pop would introduce it to one of the holes. Lifting the net he allowed the animal to slip eagerly, yet silently, into the subway that led to the underground world of the rabbits. Properly a female ferret is known as a gill, the male a hob. Pop referred to them as does and bucks, and out of deference to him I will conform to his terminology.

It was a doe ferret that was always put to use first. Once the rabbits were aware of its deadly presence a mass exodus ensued. The terrified creatures ran slap into the outspread nets where, completely enmeshed and helpless, they were quickly dispatched, each by way of a deftly delivered broken neck.

217

All nets were replaced as soon as possible, but if a rabbit were to bolt whilst another was being dealt with at the same hole, or perhaps slip away from a hitherto undetected exit, there was Pop waiting at a judicious range ready with his twelve-bore.

This was the general run of things, but there were very often snags — even with the variety of predators at Pop's disposal. Sometimes when the rabbits were unusually stubborn (Pop's expression) and the ferrets inexplicably ineffective, Pop would use one of two polecats, which he kept in his small menagerie. I do not recall their sex, only their smell. Closely allied to the ferret family they were just that much more vicious than the fairly docile ferrets and were consequently handled with a little more respect.

There was one more member of this carnivorous fraternity. He, too, was brought in when things were not running well. A big buck ferret. He was known as the Liner, and whenever a member of his harem "went to ground" (this was a term indicating that, for reasons best known to herself, a doe had decided to remain underground and inert) he would be sent down to locate her.

The Liner wore a collar to which was attached a length of strong cord. His approach did not always prompt her to move, but if he remained with her, and he usually did, one was able to establish roughly their whereabouts by measuring the amount of cord taken up by the buck's progress and then assessing the fall and direction of the tunnel.

218

Having ascertained the likely position, the next step was to dig down very carefully with the spade that was always carried for such a contingency. By a quirk of fate this seemed to occur mostly on a Sunday morning and always near noon just before the pub opened. Pop and Father would toil like navvies in their efforts to find the Liner, but it had to be done with some form of restraint, otherwise a couple of ferrets might well have been sacrificed in honour of Bacchus.

My father, after a little while without any signs of success, almost always came out with the same lament. "I'll 'ave to leave you for a few minutes, Pop. I must slip to the Half Moon to get some baccy."

Pop was nobody's fool, but amiable to a high degree. "That's alright, Jack," he would say, "I'll slip off an' 'ave my pint as soon as you get back." With his pipe firmly clenched between his worn teeth, he would go on with a smile. "These bloody ferrets must know when it's Sunday dinner-time. Aggravatin' sods."

On weekend afternoons Harry and I would often accompany Pop on his regular traipse to the piggery, which was a fair distance away across a couple of undulating and very big fields. He was responsible for the welfare of about twenty pigs. It took Pop some thirty minutes to give them their meal, a little less if we lent a hand. But it was not the pigs that interested us so much. It was the fact that Pop nearly always carried his twelve-bore with him. There were plenty of rabbits around, especially if it were near sundown, so that there

219

was always the likelihood of a little sport: at that time, my sentiments not those of the poor rabbits.

The twelve-bore was an odd-looking gun, mainly because of its inordinately long barrel. It was very old and the time-polished stock was said to be that of a Boer War rifle. A clever gunsmith had replaced the rifled barrel with the present long, smooth shotgun barrel. It was bolt-actioned, long-ranged, and it kicked like a mule.

Years later, long after we had left school, because the barrel was worn so thin, constituting a very dangerous risk when being fired, we sawed a good eight inches off the muzzle, and still the gun was as effective as ever.

Pop would sometimes pick off a rabbit or two while crossing the fields, but the most likely place for an easy kill was the little yard in the middle of the piggery. Our approach to this was from high overlooking ground. Peeping over a hedgerow, fortuitously growing in just the right position on the final downward slope of the land, we obtained a panoramic view of this little yard. If sundown were nearing, it would very often be teeming with rabbits all intent upon an early nocturnal meal. But at any time, if one made a stealthy approach to the hedge, there was always a firm likelihood of there being more than one furry target.

With a bit of luck there was a fair chance that one might hit two or even three rabbits with a single shot. Luck played its part in the way the rabbits positioned themselves. By even momentarily gathering closely, a brace or perhaps a trio of them would present one perfect target. Bear in mind the moment the gun was fired, the immediate surroundings were instantly devoid of rabbit life. All survivors had gone underground in a flash, and they stayed that way for a considerable time. It did not pay to miss.

One evening in late spring Pop allowed me to take my first shot. Harry had already fired on a number of occasions, with mostly good results. I, being just that much younger and smaller, had been made to wait. I was soon to learn the wisdom of this. But just then it was my turn.

With Pop and Harry standing a yard or so behind me, I nervously peered over the hedge. I was in luck the yard was crowded with rabbits. I pointed the gun to where they were thickest and, with closed eyes, I fired.

In a trice, a flash, a bang, and I was lying upon the ground looking up at the evening sky. The recoil had knocked me off my feet, and I thought for a moment my shoulder had been shattered. Seeing that I was unhurt, albeit white-faced and not a little shaken, Pop and Harry roared with laughter. Well, I suppose it was funny to them.

Before I regained whatever composure a youngster of twelve is supposed to possess, having fired a weapon with a recoil which felt like that of a sixteen inch gun, Harry reported that I had bagged three rabbits. I never bettered that, nor did I equal it often, and I never held a gun to my shoulder so loosely again.

There was one other animal belonging to Pop's menagerie, for I think it might well have been included

221

in a category of wild beasts. It was Tugs, the strongest and toughest looking dog I have ever seen. If he were made up of all the proverbial fifty-seven varieties, then they had all surely been Tarzans of the canine world.

In general appearance, I suppose he reminded one of a cross between a boxer and a bull terrier. His kennel was the interior of a large shed and even there he was held by a heavy iron chain. As a watchdog he was superb, and he had little need to resort to high-powered barking, for the noise he created would raise the scalp of any would-be prowler. It was more of a roar than a growl: a terrifying, chilling sound that might well prompt one to suspect that his lineage included the infusion of lion's blood.

He was genuine, too. Given less than half a chance he would happily dispose of any doubts regarding his belligerent nature. He was allowed off the chain only in the company of Pop, for he was a one master dog, responding to Pop, and Pop alone.

Tugs was friendly towards Harry, and he grew to tolerate my father, Cecil and me, but only just. Anyone else who entered Pop's garden felt in jeopardy, for the shed door was mostly open, and even the sight of that thick chain was not completely reassuring. One feared that the staple to which it was attached might easily, under such strain, part company with the wall into which it was cemented.

In fact, at a later date this occurred.

CHAPTER
TWENTY

The Fire-Raiser

Not all of my childhood memories which include animals are about indigenous creatures. A tale of happy coincidence was brought about by two large beasts from a far distant clime. It happened at a time when part of our school gardens was in dire need of a fertilizer. The man who instructed us on Monday afternoons woefully and repeatedly declared, "We need a hefty load of good manure on that soil, or it won't produce a ruddy thing."

Mr. Purser agreed, and the school authorities were sympathetic, but were unable to extend financial aid during the current fiscal year. They pointed out that they had earlier that year purchased a large load of manure from a local farmer, and that there had also been the additional expense of buying a dozen new spades. There was to be no help from that quarter.

"I s'pose we'll 'ave to dig that bit over next week," grumbled our instructor, "But it'll be a complete waste of time."

As I have mentioned, the school gardens were at the top extreme of the meadow, and the juniors' football pitch at the opposite lower end. This was not marked out and during the summer months, except for the juniors using a small area of it for softball cricket, it was nothing more than a piece of waste land, grazed upon, whenever the grass looked tempting enough, by our old friend the pony.

There were rare occasions when this part of the meadow was hired by a funfair or a circus. There were then far more of these itinerate entertainments than today and if, for some reason, a field was unobtainable nearer the town, the school meadow was considered second best. It was during a morning playtime that a circus, coming from the direction of Midhurst, passed by our school on its way to the meadow.

Steam vehicles pulling canvas-draped cages and wagons that were stacked high with all the gaudy paraphernalia associated with amusements such as this puffed their way to the turning into June Lane and into the meadow. Bringing up the rear were two elephants, lumbering along line astern. I will never know whether they were just being exercised or, indeed, had walked all the way from their previous venue.

Mr. Purser had joined us in the playground and although, officially, our time was up, he extended the period so that we might watch all of the procession finally come to a halt in the field.

The elephants were some way behind and the leading one had just reached a point in the road opposite to where we were grouped on the playground when it was compelled to answer the call of nature. This seemed to have an auto-suggestive effect upon the trailing animal for, moving slightly out of line, it, too, was compelled or perhaps it simply decided to follow the leader's example. One could hardly say it was as though molehills appeared on the road, more like mountains, I would say.

Mr. Purser's evaluation of the situation was instant. "By Jove, boys," he cried, "They've dropped their luggage!" He went on excitedly, "Quick, lads, we need buckets, sacks and shovels. Get it to the school gardens right away."

The transportation of the much-desired manure was soon in operation. Many hands make light work and there was no shortage of volunteers, for everyone concerned was able to avail himself of a close-up view of the circus on his way to and from the garden. That alone was worth the labour.

That was not the end of the matter. Mr. Purser came to an arrangement with the circus boss and when the whole show moved on, after only a few days, in the corner of the school garden there was a huge mound of manure. Our gardening mentor was delighted.

I have described the idyllic surroundings of the school grounds. But there was one potential drawback. Should there be a common-fire in the near vicinity, it must ever pose a threat to the school itself.

After a spell of dry windy weather, but not necessarily hot, a carelessly discarded match or cigarette end falling upon tinder-dry undergrowth would be enough to cause a terrific fire, sometimes in a matter of minutes. On a cloudless day, a piece of broken glass, by concentrating the sun's heat on to any dry material, produced the same effect.

Whatever the cause, the end result was much the same: acres of nothing but charred desolation. It has never failed to amaze me how quickly green shoots of countless species of vegetation poked irresistibly through a carpet of thick, black ash.

On rare occasions, under his direction, Mr. Purser called upon those of us considered to be responsible enough and physically able to keep a fire at bay until the local volunteer fire brigade arrived.

Some of us were armed with what at a glance looked like huge besom brooms. In reality, heavy bundles of twigs wired to the ends of stout poles, a device made specifically for beating out flames by members of the woodwork class. Others carried large wet sacks to be used in the same way.

I have never decided which of these two fire-fighting instruments was more effective. I do know one was more likely to get one's hair and eyebrows singed when using a damp sack, for to use it efficiently entailed standing upon the very threshold of the fire, whereas beating down the blaze with a bundle of twigs attached to the end of a pole did not require one to get in quite so close.

It all seems very alarming, but we, the fire fighters, were never in any real danger, even when the fire forced a sudden retreat by the intervention of its ally the wind. Since we were primarily concerned with the protection of the school, we could only be driven back towards it and, at worst, be forced to cross the main road to find complete safety.

I know that amongst us there were those who enjoyed fire fighting, and who had no real desire to see the blaze put out. To them it was a pleasant diversion from lessons and, so far as they were concerned, if the school went up in smoke — so what? We might be given a long holiday. There were others like myself who I am sure would have fought to preserve the school at all cost, simply because we loved the old place and all that it stood for.

There was a third element who hated school, and all that it stood for, to that very same degree. They were in the minority, and my loyalty to the school was evident to these few, so that I remained unaware of the skulduggery going on at the time. Many years were to pass before the facts were bit by bit revealed.

It seems that in the main the fires, which occurred near the school were deliberately started by a boy or boys for whom school was a disagreeable imposition. If conditions were favourable and the wind in the right direction, they would kindle a fire with a match or a magnifying glass, usually during playtime or a dinner break, and then run off hoping for the best. There is no doubt in my mind that these assertions, and even confessions reaching my ears over the passing years, are true.

The school building was converted into private dwellings several years ago. Prior to that for over thirty years it remained in use as a primary school only, which means that there were no longer any "big boys" attending. I still live close to the old school site, and in all those years I have not seen a common-fire anywhere near the place. Yet they were once so frequent.

One morning there was a particularly large fire, some way off, but heading towards the school from the direction of a beautiful spot called Sunset Hill. At least it had been beautiful a short time earlier.

Of that once lovely headland, where there had been heather and gorse and a diffusion of young silver birch, interspersed with pathways surfaced with generations of pine needles, there was nothing but a layer of smoking ash. Incredibly, the great pine trees were still alive. They seemed to reach for the cool of the heavens. Alive, and looking proudly defiant despite their blackened trunks and their charred and naked lower limbs.

But for that area, it was the aftermath. We were concerned with the line of all-devouring flames, which swept upon us from that direction. Animals of all kinds, large and small, even snakes, were running or slithering away in sheer terror. There were a lot of adders on the common in those days, so we watched where we stepped. A lot of the snakes made the mistake of first going to ground, only to find the heat becoming unbearable, before fleeing for their lives all too late. They were literally cooked alive. After a fire had burned out and the earth grown cool enough to walk upon, we always found the remains of a lot of reptiles, mostly fused to the ground and in a brittle condition.

This day was no exception. I was not terribly sorry for the snakes; since that distant day amid the primroses I had ever regarded them with a feeling of revulsion. I was sorry for the birds, squirrels and rabbits. They would all most likely survive, but they were rendered homeless by a few seconds of searing heat.

The rabbits might gain the sanctuary of an alien, but friendly, burrow and merely wait until things cooled off before returning home. Whatever the lodging accommodation one thing was certain, when it came to seeking food many parts of unburnt common would become highly over-populated.

The wind blew steadily from the west and we lads, the vanguard of the fire fighters on that morning, along with all living creatures, retreated eastwards. An isolated house called The Cherries was in real danger for the fire brigade had failed to turn up, even after a second call. The reason, we later learned, was that they were engaged with a similar fire elsewhere.

Reaching up at the young trees, the flames towered above us, at times to a height of fifteen feet or more, and there was nothing we could do but fall back. We were at the gateway to The Cherries and so, too, was the fire when the helmets and hoses and very appreciative men arrived upon the scene.

We were dismissed at once, but not without their praises ringing loudly and ungrudgingly in our young and sooty ears. With their hoses they soon forced the fire away from the house, but it was a long time before the blaze was completely put out.

★　★　★

Returning to the seat of learning, feeling very brave and a little dirty, I must confess that, as much as I liked school, there was a certain dullness to life after fighting a fire like that.

During the early afternoon there came another fire alarm and clearly this was a conflagration much nearer the school. We, the morning campaigners, were called upon once more, and this time we actually put out the fire before the official fire fighters came along and damped down the embers.

We were complimented by the fire chief, but about a quarter of an acre of thick vegetation had been destroyed before we won the day, and it was all perilously close to the back of the school.

Nearly fifty years later I was to learn how this particular fire was started and the name of the culprit. Over a quiet drink (out of prudent respect I will use only the initial letter of his Christian name) J told me it was he who started that one, with the help of a box of matches. His nefarious plan could so easily have succeeded, and he went on to say that at the time he was bitterly disappointed, for he was going through a period of his young life when school and everything about it was objectionable. Seeing the threat to The Cherries in the morning had sparked off an idea that might well have resulted in a flaming success, at any rate that was J's opinion at the time.

CHAPTER
TWENTY-ONE

The Midhurst Musketeers

Outside of sport, the sort of games we boys generally played at came round in cycles. This was influenced by whatever type of adventure film had last appeared at the local cinema. A tale about swashbuckling pirates would produce a game requiring a show of sensibly blunt wooden cutlasses. A game based upon a saga of deepest Africa would involve the production of rather dangerously pointed spears. Thin wooden rapiers with ornamental guards, usually made of painted cardboard, would be inspired by a "Three Musketeer" kind of film. Plenty of cheap metal cap guns were toted around after a gangster or western feature: the latter needing also the production of several bows and lots of arrows.

Most certainly, the bow and arrow was the favourite homemade weapon. Harry and I possessed several bows, most of them made of ash; there were few yew trees on our side of Midhurst. Both of us could be classified as senior boys of the local play gang, I was twelve and Harry just short of thirteen. We were both a little bigger and that much stronger than the rest of the kids around us. In consequence of this our bows were easily the most powerful in the community. Come to think of it, we were probably not so strong as we thought, for it sometimes took either of us all of his strength to pull back a newly made bow. Youngsters, please note. When a bow requires that much effort, it is a very dangerous toy.

We tried all sorts of ways to produce a lasting point at the business end of the arrows, from charring the tip in fire to fitting the heads of old featherless darts to the end of the shaft. This attachment provided a needle-sharp point, which, having been fired from one of our bows, was unfortunately most difficult to retrieve should it be found embedded in a tree or barn door.

That there were times both Harry and I underestimated the lethal power of our bows is now freely acknowledged by both of us. But in those days, everything was experimental and we learned by our mistakes: two of which were very nearly fatal.

It was harvest time 1936 that I came, literally, to within an eighth of an inch from a manslaughter charge. It was at the end of a beautiful day. Away to the west the sun was foundering in a red and amber sea of broken cloud. Harry, Cecil and I were about to wend our way home. All evening we had been at archery practice in a field of stubble, using cardboard targets placed against the side of a hayrick.

Harry and I had gathered up our bits and pieces, but Cecil was still looking for a missing arrow. We left him to it and slowly moved away. As we headed towards the gate of the barnyard, which led to June Lane, Cecil, having found the arrow, fired a rather innocuous shaft in our direction. It was only done in fun, and screaming in mock defiance he took refuge behind a loosely packed bale of hay, where he noisily awaited our certain retribution. Harry had already unstrung his bow, so it was left to me to return fire.

That is how it started, but soon the excitement mounted and Harry restrung his bow and joined in. We were using wooden tipped arrows, not very sharp, and we were not drawing our bows to any great extent. Short of catching a shaft in the eye, it was not particularly dangerous. Cecil sent the occasional arrow towards us, but in the main we pinned him down with fairly accurate shots into and around the straw bale.

I suppose we played like this for about five minutes, and then Cecil, who by then had run out of arrows and dare not reach out for the ones stuck in the ground around him, decided to charge. Bearing in front of him the bale of straw for protection, and uttering a fearsome cry, he rushed towards us. At a range of some twenty paces I levelled an arrow, and totally underestimating the penetrative powers of a slender shaft through loosely packed straw, drew my bow fairly hard, aimed at the centre of the bale, and let fly.

The arrow plunged into the straw. Cecil stopped abruptly and the bale fell to the ground. At that distance, with the sunset faded into twilight, we watched appalled as he tottered backwards over the stubble with an arrow protruding from just above his

Adam's apple. He fell to the ground and lay motionless upon his back.

Oh, my God! What had I done?

As we rushed to him, the arrow dropped slowly sideways, the feathered flight rested upon the stubble, but the point remained embedded in poor Cecil.

We reached him and saw in an instant that the arrow had penetrated the bone under the point of his jaw. An eighth of an inch lower — perhaps even less — and that arrow must have buried itself in his throat. As it was, it had virtually knocked him out. With waves of relief sweeping over us — especially me, the guilty one — Harry and I hauled Cecil to his feet. The arrow was removed very easily, but then came the blood. It gushed out.

My father had warned us all repeatedly of the dangers of playing with toys such as homemade bows and arrows. We could be sure of a rough reception from him. Better go to Harry's house and try to stop the bleeding.

In the gathering gloom we arrived unseen. Pop had already gone for his nightly "noggin", as he called it, so the coast was clear for us to put all our medical expertise into practice. To hold Cecil's chin under a running cold-water tap proved to be our limit in this field, but after what seemed hours, it actually worked. The bleeding stopped.

Pop had never bothered with wireless, so, of late, Harry was in the habit of coming over to my place at the end of an evening just to sit and listen to the radio with me and the family. He reminded me that one of our favourite programmes was due to begin in five minutes' time.

Cecil seemed to have made a good recovery. He had looked pretty pale for a while, but there was a familiar touch of colour back in his cheeks. "I'm alright," he said, glancing once more at the mirror. "As long as there's no more blood, I'll keep my chin tucked in and it won't be seen."

Not bad, I thought, for a kid of eight.

We crossed the road and made for the flat, both Harry and I peeped apprehensively through the dim light of a distant street-lamp at poor old Cecil's jaw. So far, so good. Without putting on the light we clattered up the stairs to the flat and turned into the front room.

Father and Mother, one either side of the fireplace, were seated listening to the radio. Both looked up as we entered. Mother had to look over her shoulder at us; Father looked straight across at us, and it was his expression that changed first.

"What the hell . . ." was as much as Father said at that moment. He was staring at Cecil, for the wound had reopened and blood was pouring all over the place. It might have been due to the exertion of climbing the stairs, but, whatever the reason, Mother immediately took over, ushering Cecil to the bathroom. Mother was a nurse by birth, as many a grateful neighbour had remarked.

Although Father professed little time for "books and things", he was a shrewd man and not easily fooled. "Ruddy bows an' arrows, I suppose?" He had posed a question, but his tone of voice demanded no less than affirmation. And, by hitting the head of the nail so accurately, he rendered us speechless, thereby depriving us of any chance to lie our way out of trouble.

Cecil's wound could have been inflicted in a thousand different ways, but from his garden earlier in the evening Father had seen us with our bows and arrows and since he hated to see us using "those weapons", it was an inspired guess. Our total lack of argument gave to him the proof he needed. What he was about to do he had had in mind for a long time, justification had been presented.

He stormed his way out of the room, grabbing a pocket torch from the sideboard as he swept by. He looked as mad then as he did on the morning he sent me to see Rev. Tatchell.

The radio had been silenced and from across the road came the sound of Tugs roaring for a confrontation in his usual ferocious manner. Then came silence, indicating that Father had conciliated the dog very quickly. We knew what was happening. The whole of our armoury of bows and arrows was stored in that kennel-cum-shed. Father, without laying a hand upon us, was in the process of teaching us a very tough object lesson.

In the morning we surveyed the debris. Every item in our store of archery requisites had been broken into small pieces.

I was not too upset about it; it was something I knew I deserved. I still felt numb with relief at knowing Cecil was alive. I could not speak for him nor for Harry; after all, one was the victim and the other was innocent.

Even now, nearly half a century on, a cold sweat is not far off whenever I recall the horrifying moment that I thought Cecil had been mortally wounded.

And yet, less than one year after that fright, Harry and I were still making all sorts of arrows to be fired from even more powerful bows. Father appeared to have relented just a little, but we were extremely careful to adhere to target shooting only, if he were anywhere around.

One summer evening Harry and I were standing high in a field, which swept upwards very steeply from the back garden of Pop's house. We were about to test a new bow. The arrow to be discharged was of the dart-tipped variety, shouldered with a heavy lead weight. We calculated that by firing the shaft almost vertically into the air, it should come to rest at a point somewhere at the far end of a small meadow, which lay a long way off on the other side of the house.

Harry, who was probably the strongest boy in our locality, drew that bow with every ounce of his strength and with a vicious twang of the bowstring the arrow was on its way. The angle of release was just right, so far as the trajectory was concerned, the trouble was that the arrow had taken a north-westerly course instead of flying due west.

Away it sped, up and ever upwards, far above the row of tall pines, which stood like sentinels guarding the boundary of Pop's back garden and the lower rim of the field. Still climbing until it was no more than a black dot against the light blue of the evening sky. It was easily the highest altitude we had ever attained with an arrow. No more than a speck in the heavens, the arrow seemed to hover for a moment before beginning its descent of ever increasing velocity.

We quickly estimated that it was diving straight for the hard metalled surface of June Lane, just behind the Half Moon gardens. That was unfortunate, for the thin steel point would probably snap on impact, even if the arrow remained intact. As we watched it plummeting earthwards we could see its chicken-feathered flight spinning madly. Another movement caught our attention. An elderly lady, one of our new, near neighbours, Mrs. Pollard by name, had appeared upon that stretch of the lane. She sauntered along in the evening sunshine, a short, white-haired figure following a long shadow, totally unaware of imminent danger from above. With bated breath we watched the final course of the arrow. It was all over in seconds, but it seemed an eternity.

The steel-headed shaft struck the centre of the road not more than six feet behind her. She ambled on not hearing the thud, for she was, fortunately for her peace of mind at that moment, slightly deaf.

Harry and I raced down the hill as one, through Pop's garden and into June Lane. To retrieve that arrow before anybody saw it protruding from the road was our single objective. We knew the depth of trouble we would most certainly be in should someone report our latest performance of highly dangerous tomfoolery, especially if Father were to hear.

So far as we know there was no witness as we pulled the arrow from the road. The point of the shaft was surprisingly undamaged and we retrieved it after some considerable effort. Its entire length, about an inch and a half, had buried itself in that metalled surface. We discussed whether or not Mrs. Pollard's skull was as tough as the road.

All young archers, take heed. These events demonstrate the lethal power that can be released by a straining cord, which for a brief moment has been instrumental in bending a length of wood far in excess of its natural curvature. With what eagerness it regains its normal shape!

CHAPTER
TWENTY-TWO

The Air Raid Shelter

By the end of 1936 we had been ruled by three consecutive monarchs, the mighty Crystal Palace had been destroyed by fire (I still feel a sad affinity with that piece of history) and the newspapers, along with our schoolteachers, acknowledged the futility of Abyssinian spears against the armoured cars of Italy. Civil war had broken out in Spain and east of the Maginot Line war clouds loomed upon the horizon.

By January 1937, when I began my first term directly under Mr. Purser, I was aware that a few suspicious fingers were already pointed towards Germany. My father always insisted that, if there were to be a war, this time we would fight with the Germans against the Bolsheviks. Mr. Purser disagreed with this theory; he did not trust Hitler, and he said so, very often, in no uncertain manner. He told us once that he shared the sentiments of a certain Mr. W. S. Churchill and wished there were more about like him.

Perhaps the threat of war created more employment, for even in little, rural Midhurst the dole queues continued to steadily shrink, and the standard of living grew accordingly better for a great many of us.

Improved housing conditions, adequate clothing and earlier recourse to medical advice were chief factors already making a mark upon the general health of everybody concerned. Even "Nitty Nora", the nurse who periodically visited the school and ran a fine comb through everyone's hair, must have found it increasingly difficult to justify that aspect of her profession.

Compared to the way we fared in those early days we, as a family, enjoyed astoundingly good health. The exception was that both Cecil and I continued to suffer from intermittent and painful bouts of earache.

By this time, newsreels showing the devastation of aerial bombardments, chiefly on the Spanish front, were included in all cinema programmes. This prompted Harry and me to prepare our own haven of refuge in good time. With the help of Cecil we constructed an air-raid shelter.

We selected a piece of waste ground, quite near the ferret cages, to the June Lane side of Pop's garden. Here we first excavated a nice big hole, some six feet deep and six feet square. We then procured, whether by fair means or foul I do not recall, a very strong wooden beam, which satisfactorily spanned the hole and supported a roof made up of old weatherboards and rust-encrusted corrugated iron, covered deeply with all the surplus soil. Since the weatherboards had fallen from the sides of a nearby barn and were therefore serving no purpose at all, we did not consider ourselves guilty of theft. The corrugated iron we found at the local refuse tip.

241

The entrance to the shelter was below ground level and reached by a steeply sloped trench. We were well satisfied with our achievement and every adult who examined it, even war veterans, congratulated us. I feel that their examination must have been of a cursory nature, especially in the light of subsequent events.

Fortunately, at that time we had no occasion to use it for its original purpose and after a short spell we used it as a subterranean camp. From it we dug a couple of narrow tunnels, which came to the surface several yards away at "secret" places obscured by undergrowth, which everybody knew had been deliberately placed in order to conceal the entrances. There is no doubt we had a lot of fun playing in and around that shelter. Finally, it was used as a dungeon for the prisoners taken in our war games. War being the operative word.

Many of the new council houses adjacent to the flats contained families, which boasted of at least a couple of boys, so there was a big increase in the local young male population. The games we played were much the same as described earlier, except that they were on a much larger scale and, perhaps because we were growing older, very much rougher.

Many of the cheap toy guns were replaced with airguns: another sign, maybe, of the improving affluence of local society. Usually we would split up into two gangs, one armed with mostly airguns and the other with bows and arrows. That no one was seriously injured puzzles me to this day. Arrows and pellets flew thick and fast, sometimes nearly all day long. I suppose the answer must lie in the fact that the arrows were not

242

sharply pointed and the airguns not very powerful. Nevertheless, that so many pairs of young eyes remained intact is little short of a miracle. One lad did get a pellet in the eye, but it did no permanent damage. This accident scared and subdued us for at least a couple of days.

Cecil and I kept a low profile whenever Father appeared in the vicinity of these games, and when the sport had ended for the day we hid our bows and arrows, along with Harry's, down in the dugout.

The dugout, which was by then the term everybody used when referring to the one-time air-raid shelter, could accommodate five or six youngsters quite easily and on many occasions we held just such a number of prisoners underground for quite long spells. Tugs made a very efficient guard. He was chained to a tree with enough freedom of movement to permit him to reach all three exits. Under this arrangement no one ever escaped.

Very few lads volunteered to become prisoners, quite understandably, so some of the hand-to-hand fighting was vicious and dangerous, heavy quarter-staffs being used, discolouring many a fingernail by a sudden and not always unintended contact. To be thrown shirtless into a bed of nettles was a common torture, as was being spread-eagled to a tree and flogged with a switch. There were times when an over-zealous application of the latter punishment brought the wrath of an offended parent down on the administrator's head, but such an incident had no lasting effect and we carried on playing in the same enthusiastic way.

243

We played so violently we worked an innate belligerency out of our systems. In all the years that followed those school days I have not heard of a single act of brutality levelled against any one of the kids I knew so well.

January of that year produced a lot of rain, and on a particular Sunday afternoon (I still attended the Methodist Chapel in the morning) Harry and I kept four or five prisoners underground for at least a couple of hours, despite their complaints about water seeping in from the sides of the dugout. It was around three-thirty that we released them.

Twenty-four hours later the dugout roof caved in.

We kids were all at school, but we later received graphic accounts of the calamity from the tenants of the block of flats immediately opposite the one-time air-raid shelter. Several of them had heard a muffled squelching sound, which had drawn their attention to the tail end of the incident. But there was one witness who had seen it all, mud and water thrown high in the air as, without warning, the whole lot fell in. The saturated walls of earth, which alone supported the heavy crossbeam, had caved in causing the roof to drop instantly under the weight of tons of wet soil.

We hardly dared envisage what might have occurred, nay, what would have occurred, had that roof collapsed twenty-four hours earlier.

Uncle Mossy often strolled up from Duck Lane and paid us a visit. At the time of the incident he was having a cup of tea with my mother, but neither of them heard or saw anything of the collapse until the news spread through the flats. He made for the scene at once.

Seeing further danger he quickly filled in the tunnels and levelled the site, leaving everything safe and tidy. That is the way it was when we kids arrived from school and crowded around the muddy patch, which shortly before had been our dugout. We stood and gazed, open-mouthed, strangely silent, each with a common thought in mind.

For Harry and me this event proved a milestone in our lives. It ended our participation in those rather mad games. It was not the near disaster in itself that prompted this. It was simply that we had entered another stage in the process of growing up.

At this point in our young lives we left a part of our childhood behind. We had lost the urge to play games of pretence. Already life was demanding a more realistic approach.

Our bows and arrows lay buried under that wet earth, gone forever with that essence of young life, which gave us sparkling, vigorous fantasies and leaves us with dulled yet quietly amusing memories to take with us through the sands of time. Rather like an earlier occasion when I finally and reluctantly admitted to myself the non-existence of Santa Claus. Yet the memory of his visits still remains.

We did not entirely disassociate ourselves with the youngsters of June Lane. There was always the game of football to be enjoyed, and we were fortunate in being allowed to use the school pitch, goal posts as well.

Nor were Harry and I inseparable pals by any means. He still attended his tiny village school and remained close to a lot of his old friends who would from time to time pay him a visit, and vice versa.

Along with several children of the June Lane community I continued to attend "Bright Hour" at the Methodist Hall, which, as ever, was held upon Wednesday evening. Harry never once accompanied me; it simply did not appeal to him. But it did attract a lot of kids of all age groups: most enjoyable, too, for, despite the cinema and wireless, we were still in the era of do-it-yourself entertainment. It was here, too, that each week I would meet up with some of my former pals of Duck Lane, although by this time there were considerably fewer of them still residing in the lane.

Nevertheless, Harry and I spent a good deal of time together. We had by then entered what I can only refer to as our mechanical age. Harry was the first of the June Lane lads to possess and maintain a bicycle. He needed it to cut the time, if not the distance, of his daily journey to school and back.

Half a mile or so across the common, which lay behind my school, was the local refuse tip. A veritable supply base when it came to securing spare parts for cycles. Harry, who was the number one mechanic in our juvenile community, seldom bought replacements for his bicycle; spare parts could usually be found by searching through the rubbish dump with the aid of nothing more than a full set of spanners. Almost everything required to make up a bicycle was to be found there, with the exception of tubes and tyres, although we did once or twice come across a tyre with just a little wear remaining.

In consequence of all this I eventually became the owner of a bicycle myself. It was a hybrid-plus model to be sure, but it ran all right; a fact that was solely attributable to Harry, for he created it single-handed, I being as poor a mechanic as he was good. It was amazing what we found on that filthy dump. Perhaps it was another sign of improving times. The kennel-cum-shed still occupied by Tugs was bestrewn with cycle spare parts and spanners where once had lain bows and arrows.

At about this time there was another change in the offing, a significant and deserved one for Pop. Pop was one of the most even-tempered men I have ever known. Yet, as with all of us, there were moments when he was unable to restrain himself and a torrent of expletives would seemingly assuage a provocation. But it always occurred in the same highly amusing manner.

I will record the very first time I witnessed this, for, young though I was, it amazed me in a most humorous way. I was to learn that such a reaction was absolutely typical of Pop, whatever the irritation or, indeed, pain.

No matter the task in hand, Pop had a rather nice habit of humming to himself. I remember on this occasion he was chopping kindling wood in the doorway of Tugs's shed. As usual, he was humming away when a piece of wood flew up and struck him violently on the nose. For a second, despite my youthful presence, profane oaths rained through the air like hail from the heavens. And then, as if there had been no intermission at all, he resumed humming on precisely the note he had abandoned a moment before, still chopping wood and blinking through the tears.

Whether it was an innate stoicism, an inbred philosophy, or just a habit developed perhaps by the discovery that such a response helped alleviate whatever distressed him, I know not. But a like reaction to adversity or pain I never saw in another to this day.

Since the death of his wife, life for Pop had been hard. He worked long hours on the farm, which, because of pig feeding, included turning out on every day of the year. Pigs get hungry, even on Christmas Day. Remember there were not, as yet, statutory annual holidays. Every day of the year meant just that.

He had a large garden to contend with; Harry helped him with that and with some of the housework, but then there was always the cooking to be done. Every evening Pop would heap vegetables along with pieces of meat into one big pot and therein cook the main meal of the day. Leaving it to take care of itself upon the black hob to one side of the fire, he would then go off to do a spot of gardening, timing his return to near perfection.

I often joined them at their evening meal and, whatever culinary experts might opine regarding the use of a single cooking utensil, I can only reply that I look back over the years with mouth-watering recollections of sitting at Pop's table eating masses of boiled vegetables, and thoroughly enjoying it, even though I had already eaten my main meal of the day.

After the washing-up was done Pop usually read the daily paper, it was the first chance he had had all day, before taking himself off to the Half Moon for his well-earned pint or two.

Nan used to visit us often for tea at the flat, and it was customary for her and my parents to adjourn to the Half Moon, where they would spend a pleasant hour or so together before she left for Duck Lane. It was thus she became acquainted with Pop.

Soon, whenever they met at the pub, there was no disguising the fact that Nan and Pop were becoming increasingly friendly and it was no surprise to the observant locals when Pop began to walk Nan all the way back to Duck Lane. But there were to be many nocturnal perambulations for him before he made any real progress. Nan was cautious because of a long period of freedom following an unhappy first marriage and was not, according to Pop, easily wooed. I wondered whether or not he hummed to himself after each rebuff. His persistency paid off and at length she promised to consider his hand in marriage, but only after a spell of courtship. Not too long a time she pledged. Pop agreed most happily.

Harry, being a frequent visitor to my place, knew Nan very well and wholeheartedly approved of this favourable development.

CHAPTER
TWENTY-THREE

A School Football Match

Come May the fifth and we celebrate the crowning of George VI and Elizabeth. It would be reminiscent of the Silver Jubilee two years before. Most, if not all, of the festivities were again to take place in the grounds of the Ruins; the programme was much the same. But for me there was one notable exception.

This time my mother had acquired a fancy dress costume for me; something I was not very keen on, and over which we exchanged several cross remarks. I feel that Mother persisted because she had no wish to hurt the feelings of the person who had lent her the costume — an anonymous busybody, so far as I was concerned. Off I went to the Ruins feeling very silly in the arrow-printed rig-out of a convict. I was never angelic-looking, but at that age I would have certainly qualified more for the rôle of a choirboy than that of a hardened ruffian. And I knew it.

Down at the Ruins, just before the fancy dress parade, I sought out Father in the refreshment booth where he was enjoying a glass of beer, and made a last plea to be allowed to go home and change. But even a stimulated euphoria would not induce him to overrule Mother's decision.

He looked hard at me for a moment. "I know what it needs," he exclaimed, and wetting his palm with beer he walked over to a tent-pole and plunged his hand into the tiny mound of earth around its base. People in the tent watched with amusement as he then rubbed this muddy concoction all over my cheeks and chin.

"That's aged you a bit. Looks as though you need a shave." He brushed away the surplus mud and nodding with satisfaction returned to his beer.

I received fourth prize in the fancy dress competition. The prize was a real leather football; not a full-size one, but then neither was I, as yet.

I completely forgave both parents for having made me wear such attire, and thoroughly enjoyed the rest of the day. Perhaps parents did know best, after all.

Goodwood Week came and went; the last one for me so far as scrambling for money was concerned. Next year I would be a big boy and working for my living.

I took my last month-long holiday at Carshalton and, although in later years I spent a few days there from time to time, I was never again to meet my two pals. Bill, I believe, married during the war and moved away; Georgie was killed in that same war. There remained but two more years of peace when we exchanged farewells.

★　★　★

Returning to June Lane was nothing like so bad as returning to Duck Lane. It was not just the infinitely more salubrious surroundings, nor the superior accommodation. It went deeper than that. It was due to a standard of living, which continued to improve directly as a result of Father remaining in steady employment.

We were not, by many a yardstick, even comfortably off, but all things are relative. Cecil and I continued to share the bath water, Mother remained at her part-time job, and Father still spent many hours repairing the family footwear, not as yet being able to easily afford a cobbler's bill. We found it harder to eke out the weekly coal and coke supply.

Although central heating was a feature common to Roman domesticity, after the passing of centuries it remained an indulgence afforded mostly by the more affluent section of society. Few working-class dwellings, no matter how modern, were fitted with such a system, and our brand new flat was no exception.

There were fireplaces in two of our three bedrooms, an open fire in the living room and a solid fuel stove in the kitchen. While this was a considerable improvement upon the heating facilities we had at Duck Lane, it did require a large amount of firing to derive maximum benefit.

But Father had the assistance of his two sons and the three of us, not necessarily together, spent many contented hours gathering wood from either the common or one of the many spinneys, which intruded upon the patchwork of meadowland surrounding our home. A heavy, but transportable, length of wood was referred to as "a shoulder-stick". With pride one or other of us would stagger home and triumphantly drop a particularly large "stick" from his shoulder by the old sawhorse from Duck Lane that occupied a small corner of the little yard in front of our shed.

By way of fresh vegetables the garden did us well, but it was a big plot of land and took up a lot of Father's time. Once again he looked to his sons for support, and not in vain, although I must admit my services were never graced with enthusiasm.

In the field of entertainment, homemade wine continued to be the chief libation at a get-together of friends and family; agreeable occasions, which, I suppose because we kids were fast growing up, were becoming a little more frequent.

Always referred to as "singsongs" these parties were never rowdy and rarely disturbed other occupants in the block of flats, nor did they go on into the night to any great extent. It was a time that saw our local pubs close promptly at ten o'clock and — although I say this with tongue in cheek — God-fearing people, in accordance with country lore, should be snug in bed by the hour of eleven. In fact, if this curfew was adhered to at all, it was because most people, by nature of their rural occupations, were early risers.

I think one reason why the noise was never excessive during these singsongs was that in our flat human voices seldom vied with a musical instrument, unless it was Uncle Ern's mouth organ. He played it really well.

Sometimes Daisy and I were permitted to stay up and were even invited to join in, but as we felt a little shy in such exuberant company we were mostly satisfied with being entertained. There were rarer occasions when Cecil was allowed to be present; his claim was that he was unable to sleep because of the noise. Both Daisy and I knew it was pretence. It was curiosity alone that compelled him to remain awake. We did not blame him at all for it was a shame to miss such fun.

Marjorie, being that much younger, was usually fast asleep during these events, but there was an evening that she unexpectedly made an entrance dressed only in her nightgown. Before being led back to her bedroom, she made her debut memorable by reciting a poem, which I remember began with the line, "I was sitting on the doorstep eating bread and jam". I do not recall any more of it, but I will not forget the tremendous round of applause she received. She was six at the time.

Her contribution epitomized the whole thing. Everybody present was expected to sing or say their party-piece. The degree of talent exhibited while doing so was inconsequential: to contribute was the important thing.

As I relive those happy times, to this day I am able to place the appropriate song upon the lips of each familiar face that passes before the mind's eye. Inevitably, many of those faces are no more than memories now.

Most of the singsongs began on a Saturday evening at the Half Moon and were carried on in a quite spontaneous way with a much smaller congregation after closing time at our flat.

The ever-present homemade wine stood such an occasion in good stead, and ever-resourceful Mother always came up with sufficient bread and cheese and more than enough pickled onions. The wine and the onions seemed inexhaustible.

I always knocked back a glass or two of wine, but it did not go unnoticed and I knew both my parents were keeping tabs on me. They had yet to forget the occasion of my long sleep.

Although I truly enjoyed the wine, it was the wide variety of songs that really appealed to me. They evoked, in turn, every conceivable aspect of human emotion. The verse was sung by an individual, and everybody joined in with the chorus. Long before I left school I began to build up a fairly big repertoire of old songs, without any conscious effort whatsoever. And, even though I did not fully understand many of the words, I knew that "Burlington Bertie" was always good for a laugh; that "Just A Song At Twilight" or "Moonlight And Roses" regularly produced a mixed and transient aura of nostalgia and romance, wistfully enhanced, no doubt, by the effects of homemade wine. While "It's The Poor What 'Elps The Poor" never failed to receive murmurs and nods of approval during its actual rendition. Those might not be the correct titles, but they are the words I best remember as conveying the dedication of each song indicated.

One song puzzled me. It contained the line, "Many a Miss will be Missus some day through riding on top of a tram". My experiences of tram travel told me that it was certainly not the most comfortable means of transport. Indelible memories of sitting on rock-hard slatted seats upon open-topped trams were easily recalled. The jolting and the noise, the draughty cold — should the weather be less than summery. And once, on a wet night, it was purgatory. Not my idea of a place for romance.

So I reasoned, without the benefit of experience, that all lovers could do effectively by way of courtship on top of a tram was to sit fairly close together shouting sweet nothings through a megaphone.

Little knowing I had a lot to learn, I regarded that song with strong scepticism. ———

At school, procedures and conditions altered not one iota. I remained a keen pupil and most certainly did not look forward to leaving. I enjoyed the environment of the classroom where my chief interests were inclining towards history and, more especially, to writing essays.

Despite my love of the classroom, I looked forward eagerly to Wednesday afternoons. Not so much during the summer months, for I was never a keen cricketer. It was the autumn I welcomed and my beloved games of football. I had been in the school first eleven for the better part of three seasons, but this did not amount to much. There was not a lot of opposition in our locality, for the most part we split up and played at home amongst ourselves, drawing upon an equal number of reserves.

★ ★ ★

256

The lack of inter-school matches was due to the travel involved. There were no transport facilities at the schools' disposal and neither the education authorities, nor most of the parents, would or could defray the expense of a bus trip. We sometimes marched to one or the other of two neighbouring villages, as in turn one of them would march to us. Both of these schools were smaller than ours so we always won the game, though not necessarily by a large margin. There were some pretty tough defenders in those village teams.

It was difficult to arrange these sorts of excursions for it needed a teacher or a truly senior pupil to take responsibility for the entire party. For a variety of reasons such a person was not always readily available. When Rogate issued a challenge and invited us to visit them it was very nearly turned down: even though we found a means of crossing the first hurdle.

Rogate was a small village some five miles away on the main Petersfield Road. The distance was the first hurdle. It was certainly too far to march to play football, but then someone came up with the bright idea of cycling.

I had my "Harry-Built" model, but many of the first eleven lads had to beg and borrow from other members of the football fraternity. Those not interested in football, and who's to blame them, turned their backs upon the project, but finally everybody concerned managed to acquire a bicycle.

Having surmounted hurdle number one we began to speculate as to the strength of the Rogate team. It was only a small school, but their audacity in challenging us indicated a great faith in their side. The situation was most interesting and we were on a hiding to nothing. These are games that must be played.

We met the second hurdle. Mr. Purser declined to ride a bicycle, and the lady teachers were just not interested. The task of holding the team reins, as it were, on this occasion was considered too much for a senior pupil. A journey such as this required the guidance of a much more mature and responsible person. There was not a lot of traffic on country roads in those days, but to permit eleven young lads to ride bicycles in convoy without escort was more than Mr. Purser dared.

We had already accepted Rogate's challenge. Things looked really grim. Who was there in this whole wide world that we might call upon to undertake such an exercise?

There came to us, as it seemed from heaven itself, a Mr. Luff, a short stocky young man who lived with his wife in one of the new council houses that lay between my home and our school football pitch. His employment required shift-work hours and many times on Wednesday afternoons we footballers had seen him watching our game as he took a breather from tending his immaculate garden. Our dilemma had been brought to his notice and he immediately volunteered his services. Mr. Purser and all concerned were absolutely delighted.

Came the afternoon of truth and away we rode, shepherded all along the route by Mr. Luff. No one took liberties, no one played him up. We were all too grateful to him. We duly arrived at Rogate School's football ground. The luxury of a dressing room was unknown to us; we had biked in our football gear and, having dropped our cycles on the grass alongside the pitch, we were ready for the fray. For some reason now beyond recall, Mr. Luff was prevailed upon to act as referee.

The fact that we won the match by thirteen goals to nil was not a manifestation of Mr. Luff's partisanship, nor was it in any way a spurious reflection upon his integrity. He did in fact disallow us two or three goals, which I thought to be perfectly good ones.

The reason for our overwhelming victory was simply that we hailed from a much larger school and had, therefore, a far larger number of players from which to pick. Rogate, it would seem, had overestimated the ability of their team.

In the village, Rogate mothers gathered at the corner, knowing we had to slow down before turning into the main road home. They waited in a group, many of them with prams and pushchairs, and there they booed us loudly all the way out of the village. I suppose it was because their team had lost so heavily. We had played sportingly enough. There had been no reason to play otherwise. But the boos were not of an ugly nature, many of them emanated from smiling lips and all in all I think it was really just a bit of fun. Mr. Luff brought up the rear, cycling steadily along, showing no embarrassment and chuckling all the way as he took the corner and followed us into the main road.

There was never a return match with Rogate, although we offered them a game with our reserves. It was not that they feared another massive defeat; they were simply unable to muster a team complete with cycles. A pity; they were among the less contentious of sides.

By mentioning this sporting event I have touched upon the semi-insular way of life, which still existed in rural districts, even in those relatively modern times. After all, the train, bus and the motorcar had long since arrived.

This insularity sometimes produced a fervent local patriotism, which led, on more than a few occasions, to much more than a friendly rivalry between school football teams. It was a chauvinism kindled by the indoctrinations of previous generations who had, no doubt, lived out their lives in communities of almost complete isolation with all the attendant suspicions. There were times when a football match between two schools took on the aspect of a tribal war. But a match between the adults was sometimes worse. A number of times, the home and away matches between the senior representative teams of Midhurst and Easebourne could only be referred to as something little short of bloodbaths.

And yet I stood as a young child watching them battle it out whilst my father was explaining that relations between the two parishes had much improved since he was a young man. He told me of the great fisticuff battles that had taken place, usually on Sunday afternoons, at North Mill bridge where the parish boundary lay. Young men and teenagers from both divides confronted each other upon the bridge, each daring the opposing party to cross the border. Naturally, one side or the other took up the challenge, which resulted in attempted mayhem by all participants. Father added that Uncle Harry, as a young man, had loved it.

The demarcation line is, ironically enough, depicted by two hands, presumably about to clasp in friendship, carved in stone upon the outer side of the parapet on the bridge. I was a small child at the time Father brought this symbol to my attention, but a sense of humour was developing, for I made him laugh by saying that I thought the two hands ought to be wearing boxing-gloves. He went one better, "Knuckledusters would be nearer the mark."

But in the next few years all of this became history. The barriers of resentment and suspicion between rural communities were beginning to fall, even before I left school, to be replaced in time with a more congenial rivalry. Midhurst and Easebourne went a step further. The two parishes now boast a united team!

CHAPTER
TWENTY-FOUR

Squirrel Pie

October arrived and Harry reached his all-important fourteenth birthday. Come the end of term he was due to leave school.

There had been a bumper acorn harvest, and I bought a cheap airpistol with some of the financial proceeds. Except for initially testing it, using cardboard targets and sacrificing a few lead soldiers, I rarely handled the gun at all. I nearly threw the thing away, for it was not powerful enough to be accurate. It was a disappointment and a complete waste of money.

Cecil, who had celebrated his ninth birthday, also in October, thought otherwise. One day he borrowed it and went off to a nearby wood. A short time later he returned proudly bearing a dead grey squirrel. He admitted it was a fantastically lucky shot; at close range he had hit the poor creature in the eye, killing it instantly.

Cecil was already nearer to nature than I was, or ever would be, and in true countryman fashion, "Waste not, want not", was ever to be a maxim with him. He cooked himself a squirrel pie, ignoring the advice of "know-alls" who told him, quite erroneously, that a grey squirrel was a tree-rat. I sampled a small piece, which was all Cecil would allow me for there is not a lot of flesh required to make up a squirrel, but what there is is beautifully lean and quite palatable. I have never tasted it since.

By sheer coincidence, only a day or so later, I was to taste the flesh of yet another creature — also for the first and last time.

Near the Half Moon and adjacent to the school football pitch there was a piece of wasteland upon which, perhaps a couple of occasions each year, might be seen the colourful, horse-drawn caravan belonging to a small family of gypsies, father and mother, and one child, a lad of about my age.

From this site they plied their wares, all sorts of things ranging from clothes-pegs to little bags of lavender. They usually stayed for about a fortnight, before moving on to fields afresh.

The young lad was called Mike. He and I were quite friendly during his brief sojourns in our neighbourhood, and he was always invited to join in whenever the local boys played football on the school pitch. I think he participated in most of our activities. He reminded me of the lads around the Old Kent Road on a particular occasion a few years earlier, although Mike did wear boots, and pretty sturdy ones at that. I well recall this, for I often played football against him! Although he was very dark-skinned, with his bright eyes and white teeth he looked very clean and wholesome, despite his very shabby attire.

One evening, just as we footballers had reluctantly given best to the gathering gloom, Mike, who had not joined us on this occasion, called me over to the caravan site. "I've gotta surprise fer you." He led me to a camp-fire, which glowed with a radiance that caused the caravan doors and the little flight of steps beneath to shimmer in its light.

His mother — a pretty, dark-haired woman — came down the steps and approached the fire. With an old spade, from the deep ash in the centre of the embers, she removed what appeared to be a solid lump of clay. She broke it in two quite easily with the same implement and there, before us, lay a skinned and cooked hedgehog: the spines and skin adhering to the inner surface of the clay. The meat, which both mother and son considered to be a delicacy, was then served upon plates along with a portion of bread.

Mike did not look at me very much during the meal, being too engrossed in hedgehog flesh, but his mother, it seemed to me, seldom looked away. This was a great pity for although I do not remember the taste with any great clarity I do recall that I did not like it at all. And I sat there looking for the first opportunity to throw my piece of hedgehog into the shadow of the caravan, where I knew the white and mangy dog was tethered. At last Mike's mother left us. Mike was in the process of licking his plate with eyes closed in rapture, when I surreptitiously, though very swiftly, threw the remains of my meal to the dog. I hoped fervently that he was lurking beneath the caravan, for the last thing I wished to do was to hurt anyone's feelings. But I knew I much preferred squirrel meat, or even starling flesh, to that of a poor old flea-bitten hedgehog.

CHAPTER
TWENTY-FIVE

A Wedding in the Family

I was becoming increasingly aware that all grown-ups were not of the same generation. For the biggest part of my childhood all adults tended to look much about the same age. With the exception of really old people, with haggard features and furrowed brows who struggled along, bowed over, one hand resting on a wobbly walking-stick the other clutching at an obviously painful area of the back. In those days, so many old folk really did take on the shape of a question mark, remaining that way despite rubbing all manner of liniments into the site of the pain; treating the symptom, but not the cause. The fact is, nowadays, we see far fewer stooping figures, due, I suppose, to modern orthopaedic techniques, which must contribute greatly to keeping our aged citizens more or less upright.

Keeping the very old people in a class of their own, I had until then bundled all remaining adults into two categories, grown-up men and grown-up women. I became aware that there were several young women around, some not much older than I, and I began to realise that Fay Wray and Miss Mac were not that many years in advance of me.

My appreciative near-adolescent eye would ogle at a pretty face or linger on a silken-hosed calf, always noting whether or not the vertical seam was plumb centre. I realised there were several stages to a lifetime and I felt I was upon the threshold of the most exciting one.

But, even with this newly-acquired concept of life and age, I did not then realise that Nan was twelve years older than Pop, he being fifty-four at the time of their betrothal. They were married in the same year, upon a Saturday exactly one week from Christmas Day, 1937. The reception was held at Pop's house, which did boast a fair-sized front room. It was a delightfully happy occasion; everybody was so pleased for them. Of that party I heard only one criticism: the ladies deplored the fact that the lavatory "was a route march away at the top of the garden path".

The guests were nearly all family members, mostly on Nan's side. There was a variety of bought drinks, but the mainstay by way of liquid refreshment was without doubt the homemade wine.

A guest-artiste had been engaged; he was a local fellow who played the concertina and possessed an extensive repertoire of old songs. He had also a slight nervous affliction that caused his nose to twitch rather violently. Cecil and I found this highly amusing.

266

Whether or not there were repeated popular requests for one particular song, I know not, but one number was sung by this man at least three times during the evening; enough for me to remember these lines. And, what sentiments they conveyed upon a wedding night!

Oh I wonder, yes I wonder, will the angels way
   up yonder,
Will the angels play their harps for me?
A million miles I've travelled, and a million sights
   I've seen,
And I'm waiting for the glory soon to be.
Oh I wonder, yes I wonder, will the angels way
   up yonder,
Will the angels play their harps for me.

Nothing wrong with the song, methought, but even to a callow lad it did seem rather inappropriate at a wedding reception, especially when one considered the age of the bride!

That apart, the evening was just another enjoyable repetition of the old familiar singsong, with Uncle Ern and his mouth-organ taking over whenever the concertina man was in need of a drink and a rest.

Towards the end of the evening, during a lull in the singing, my father approached Pop and, well within the hearing of most people, asked him if he were going ferreting in the morning. The answer brought forth shrieks of laughter from all present, except from Nan

267

who, being a little deaf, merely looked around wondering what the hilarity was all about.

Pop's answer was not suitable for young ears.

Since I mentioned the subject of the happy couple's respective ages, I will broach the future. They were to remain happily married for over twenty-two years, Nan dying at the age of eighty-eight.

Christmas passed and we moved into the New Year. Harry began his working life at the local brickworks. Pop really had something to hum about then; his son was earning a living and both arrived home from work to find a waiting meal.

But a grey cloud was soon to settle on the clear horizon. Tugs was becoming more fractious than before. It is possible he might well have nurtured a certain resentment at Nan's arrival in the homestead, and she was never at ease in his presence, although he did little more than growl in her direction.

It was an extremely athletic postman who was very nearly the first victim. The shed was open and the dog, with super-canine strength, finally pulled the staple from the wall. Judged by the reports of how he cleared the garden wall, the postman ought to have been in training for the 1940 Olympic Games high jump.

Unfortunately, a week or so later, a middle-aged lady was not so lucky. Tugs, who was about to be chained to the newly-embedded staple, following a romp across the fields with Pop, completely disregarded his master's voice and managed to nip the poor woman in the leg as she hastily retreated through the garden gate. It was only a nip, for the gate had been slammed in the nick of time, almost crushing the dog's nose.

Pop could see that Tugs was becoming dangerously unmanageable. He made a heart-rending decision. As he said afterwards, it took a couple of days for him to steel himself and to carry it out. On Sunday morning, armed with his twelve-bore and a spade, Pop took Tugs for a last short walk. They crossed June Lane together and disappeared through the barnyard gates. Harry and I were standing in the shed, both of us sadly and acutely aware of the rumpled old blanket, the discarded length of chain and the unfinished bone, which lay among its own splinters, when a single shot rang out. Tug's life had ended.

Presently Pop returned, tears running, unashamedly free, damping his weather-beaten cheeks. We could see he was just about heart-broken, and we were pretty choked up, too. To Harry and me, Tug's death was yet another severed link with that wildly irresponsible period, which only a short while before had been an integral part of our lives.

We knew Tug's end had been merciful. He had not suffered at all; Pop would have made sure of that. Our old, four-legged "guard" lay buried in the barnyard.

At about this time, Harry had managed to save up enough money to purchase a really expensive air rifle. It cost thirteen shillings and sixpence (67½p) and was easily the most powerful and accurate gun of its kind in our community.

We used to take it with us on our frequent visits to the dump in quest of cycle parts. The place was crawling with rats that very sportingly offered themselves as moving targets. There were a few who virtually sacrificed themselves by approaching daringly close to the gun muzzle. We never managed to bag a really worthwhile target, like a rabbit or a pheasant, although plenty of both abounded in those days, especially on the common land surrounding the dump.

I fired head-on at a cock-pheasant on one occasion and we actually saw the pellet ricochet off the breast feathers. We were not surprised. We knew from experience that with limited power it was prudent to fire at the rear of a feathered target. At this angle the feathers are much more easily penetrated. We reckoned that if we could hit a pheasant in the head at close range it would prove fatal.

Harry had had the gun for about three months when, early one evening, I borrowed it for a specific purpose, fortunately, with his permission!

I then made for the big wych elm that stood in the far corner of a small field, which ran on from the top end of the gardens belonging to the flats. Several times just before dusk, from our kitchen window I had observed a hen-pheasant in the vicinity of this tree.

Twilight was fast approaching as I flattened myself against the massive base of the wych elm. I was just able to see over the low hawthorn hedge, from where the bird usually appeared. Silently I waited.

I knew I was doing wrong; it was a complete violation of Father's express orders never to shoot at pheasants on or over farmland. I was quite aware of the principal reason which lay behind the order, too. Father was quite friendly with Reg, the local gamekeeper, and I was old enough to realise that if I were to be caught in the act of poaching, it would be embarrassing for both of them.

But who can abide such restrictions when the hunt is on?

With loaded gun, still as the tree itself, I stood beneath the wych elm's canopy of lower branches. I had not been thus long enough to warrant the movement of a muscle, when I perceived the pheasant approaching.

Slowly I raised the rifle to the firing position and still the bird came on, padding along towards me with its familiar stiff-legged gait, and every tenth second its head grew larger in my sights. It was slightly hesitant. Come on, just a little closer and I cannot miss. My finger tightened on the trigger.

At the very moment I was about to fire, the pheasant suddenly elongated its neck as though something had caught its attention. I was totally unaware of a third presence. I was trying to line up for a second attempt when I nearly jumped out of my shoes. A voice, right at my ear said very deliberately, "Unload that gun and be quick about it."

I spun round, "Dad," I gasped, "I thought you were Reg. I had a pheasant lined up over the hedge."

The moment I spoke I realised what a serious thing I had admitted, but I need not harbour regrets over that; Father was quite conversant with the situation, having watched my little venture throughout.

"You know damned well what I've told you about shooting at pheasants," was Father's retort, and then again he gave the order, "Unload that gun and be quick about it!"

I fired the pellet harmlessly into the ground and Father grabbed the rifle from me. There was a wooden fence running through the hedge, secured at intervals to some very solid posts. Suddenly I realised my Father's intention. "But Dad! It doesn't belong . . ."

Father had already swung the gun by the barrel hard against one of the posts. The rifle had taken on the aspect of an aerial view of a U-turn.

"That'll teach you a ruddy lesson," he said angrily, throwing the then useless gun to the ground.

I stood aghast for a moment, and then finding my voice again, I blurted, "But, Dad, that isn't my gun. It's Harry's!"

For an instant, Father was taken aback; he looked almost shame-faced, but all of this lasted less than a second, and his features once more projected anger. "Then you'll have some explaining to do," came his parting comment, and he turned on his heel and strode across the field towards home.

I picked up the buckled rifle and there in the rapidly fading light I first cursed the wretched pheasant for having engaged my hunting instincts, and then began to compound an apology to Harry.

In fairness to Father, I must point out that since we lads were always swapping and borrowing all manner of items, he would be quite unable to identify the gun as not belonging to me. In his justified anger, he must be excused.

Harry was very good about it. He even raised a rueful smile as I recounted the evening's events and promised, by way of a feeble joke, that I would never borrow the gun again. At the time Harry was taking more and more interest in his father's shotgun, so despite its high price the loss of an air rifle did not grieve him overmuch. I know not what Pop said to my father about it, if anything at all, but one thing is certain, they did not fall out over it.

CHAPTER
TWENTY-SIX

Long Trousers

It was during this my last summer at school that I ceased to attend both the Methodist Chapel on Sunday mornings and the Wednesday evenings' "Bright Hour". My attendance had not been regular at either congregation since the beginning of the year and with all respect to "Bright Hour", I had felt for some time that I was getting just a little too old for the sort of games that once had given me so much pleasure.

As though to prove I was still a good Christian young lad, even though I no longer attended religious services, on my last visit to the Methodist Hall I took with me, carrying it precariously upon my bicycle saddle, the old blue pedal-car. Taking it into the hall I presented my one-time favourite toy to the man in charge of a "Gifts For Needy Children Fund".

We had all been asked to give if we were able, and the little car had long been in disuse. I had to give it a good clean: it had stood at least for a year next to the coke-heap in the shed. Cecil did not mind relinquishing ownership at all, he was far too big for it by then.

For some reason, my mother knew nothing about this donation until a short time later, when she immediately reproached me for not having given it to one of the small children who lived in the flat beneath us. I accepted this criticism, the only feeble excuse being that I just had not thought. My silly oversight actually niggled me, for my upbringing had taught me that charity began at home or as nearby as possible. And I could have saved myself the considerable effort involved in transporting the car to the hall.

I apologized to the amiable young mother of the children in question, a lady whom I considered to be very attractive despite my tender years. Little did I realise that I was talking to the woman who was to become, in the distant future, my wife.

After the departure of the car, yet another link with the Duck Lane years was to be broken. The old gramophone had for some time been no more than a cumbersome ornament resting upon the little round table, which stood in a corner of our front room. Father had several times poked about in its interior with a screwdriver, but to no avail. "Needs a new set of innards," was his final comment.

It was not so strange that one of the last records to be played on it was Father's favourite carol, "Hark the Herald Angels Sing", for it broke down on a Christmas Day and, since the radio had at once relegated the gramophone to a remote second place, Christmas Day was probably the only time it had been wound up in the last couple of years or so.

Mother decided it must go and so on refuse collection day the poor old gramophone (I felt truly sorry for it) was given into the temporary care of Aunt

275

Daisy's lodger, Bill, who still worked with the dust cart pulled by the same grey horse.

At school I was in the top standard. Mr. Purser had already explained that, because I had arrived there a little early, there would be no useful purpose served in remaining there in excess of two terms. If, therefore, there was a job open to me at the end of the second term, I might as well leave school, even though I would not be fourteen until the very end of the summer holiday.

All of this was a few months away, as yet, but there was a job in the offing. My father was acquainted with a butcher whose shop lay almost next door to Aunty Daisy's place at Church Hill. It was arranged that I would begin full-time employment at the end of Summer Term. My principal duties to begin with would be those of errand-boy, but I was also to be a trainee slaughter man as well as butcher, for all meat sold from the shop was home-killed.

The butcher already employed a Saturday morning errand-boy, a fellow of my age, named Charles. He was soon to move on, but we would do the rounds together every Saturday morning until the time came for him to depart. I was to receive two shillings (10p) for each morning's work, which I thought quite generous. After all, there were two of us doing the work of one.

Even before I began the job, I felt partly qualified. I possessed a natural urge, and the physical ability, to whistle loudly as I cycled, and that, as any self-respecting errand-boy of those days would know, was an essential attribute. I must observe that we errand-boys of yesteryear had a distinct advantage over the much-diminished ranks of our present-day counterparts. We had a steady supply of really tuneful songs, which lent themselves to all forms of rendition.

From the very outset, Charles and I got on famously together. He straddled his own machine and I rode the carrier-bike: not from choice, but because my "Harry-Built" model had recently ceased to function through lack of maintenance.

It was after Charles and I had spent at least a couple of Saturday mornings on the rounds that both of us received a most severe reprimand from the boss. I very nearly lost the job altogether or so the latter had me believing. The usual procedure when delivering an order was to politely enquire as to any future requirements. Charles had just done this and we were standing before a straight-faced, aloof-looking, middle-aged lady, giving her ostensibly all the due deference we felt she silently demanded, when finally, after much mental deliberation, she spoke. "Well, let me think," she said very slowly, "Um — Oh, I really cannot remember these days. Ah, yes, I most certainly require some brains."

Charles and I looked at each other and neither could restrain. We burst out laughing. It would seem the woman was entirely devoid of a sense of humour, for with an almost savage grimace she slammed the door in our faces.

We could do no more than go on our way, still chuckling, and unaware that she had immediately phoned the shop and reported our unseemly behaviour. It was when we arrived back from the rounds that we received our dressing-down. It was delivered to us at the rear of the shop in the shadow of the sausage machine, and it was so harsh that I think we were almost frightened to smile for quite a long time afterwards. One thing was certain, there was a vast improvement in our demeanour, which had, I admit, of late been on the slide. For me, it was lesson number one regarding my future in such an occupation: to extend nothing short of courtesy at all times.

The outcome was not bad, for the woman continued her patronage, but when we later that morning delivered the sheep brains — an order, which she had finalised over the phone — it is not just a pun to say that, as we handed them to her, we both felt and looked extremely sheepish.

Now that I was fully occupied every Saturday morning, Cecil took over the job of transporting coke, using the same old truck that I had pulled for so many years. Apart from occasional bouts of ear trouble, my brother was maintaining a much better standard of health. His stomach no longer worried him, and he was beginning to develop into a strong lad.

Marjorie, then seven, continued to enjoy the best of health, and was certainly the most robust-looking of the family. Perhaps in her case we left the squalor of Duck Lane in the nick of time.

Daisy had made a complete recovery from the effects of rheumatic fever and was still very happy in her job.

She also adds romance to the conclusion of these memoirs.

Nan and Pop had not got around to buying a wireless, so Harry continued to call upon me at the flat in order to listen to his favourite programmes. Well, that was his story, but his visits were becoming so frequent, and for such extended hours, that I felt increasingly certain there was an ulterior motive. He was losing a great deal of interest in me, of that I was sure, and it was not long before I realised that his attention was undeniably attracted towards my sister Daisy. It was also noticeable that Daisy seldom went out when she knew Harry would be calling.

And so the romance began. Quite soon I had lost the companionship of a pal, but eventually, in my late teens, I gained a brother-in-law. And I was best man on the day. Still peeping into the future, I might add, at this very time of writing, that the happy couple are about to celebrate their fortieth anniversary together.

The summer of 1938 wore on; the unwelcome school-leaving day drew near. There was, in the safe keeping of a local firm of solicitors, a charity fund bequeathed by a long-departed Mr. Ognell to assist Midhurst C of E school-leavers, provided they were resident in the parish. The amount awarded depended upon two factors: their school attendance record and their general scholastic achievements.

I feel that my poor attendance record was overlooked. But I had been a fair, all-round scholar and I know that Mr. Purser and Miss Mac gave me a high rating for my favourite subject, composition. Subsequently, I received the large award of thirty-two shillings (160p). I went along to the outfitter in West Street, where I spent the whole of this princely sum at once. I purchased a sports jacket, a pair of shoes and a pair of long trousers. All in readiness for work.

Near the end of July my final day at school arrived. One by one all school-leavers were called before Mr. Purser to receive his personal message and to exchange farewells. Sadly, I stood and listened to his advice. I wish I had heeded it, as much as I remember it. "Ron, you are leaving school to become an errand-boy. Oh, I know you might well learn a trade as a butcher, but I beg of you, never neglect that remarkable talent you have for expressing yourself in writing." The reader of this account might well ask what became of that talent. I can only suggest that all such gifts, too long neglected, become as disused tools, rusty and ineffective.

Saying goodbye to my teachers was one of the gloomiest days of my life. At the age of exactly thirteen years and eleven months, I reluctantly turned my back upon my beloved school.

The very next morning I set out for my first day's work. Confident, because I was already experienced at my job. Self-conscious because, for the first time in my life, I was wearing long trousers.